CROSSING POLECAT MOUNTAIN

Episodes in the Life of a Bumpkin

R. Linton Cox, Jr.

Crossing Polecat Mountain
Episodes in the Life of a Bumpkin
By R. Linton Cox, Jr.
Copyright@2020 R. Linton Cox, Jr.

All right reserved. This is a personal autobiographical memoir. The opinions expressed in this manuscript are solely the opinions of the author and do not represent the opinions or thoughts of the publisher. The author has represented and warranted full ownership and/or legal right to publish all the materials in this book. This book may not be reproduced, transmitted, or stored in whole or in part by any means, including graphic, electronic, or mechanical without the express written consent except in the case of brief quotations embodied in critical articles and reviews.

Cover Image: Public Domain Map
Cover Design: The Author's Mentor
Book Design and Publishing Assistant, The Author's Mentor, a subsidiary of Little Roni Publishers LLC
www.TheAuthorsMentor.com

ISBN: 9798563246898
Also available in eBook publication.

PUBLISHED IN THE UNITED STATES OF AMERICA

DEDICATION

In editing this book, my grandfather's memoir, my original plan was to dedicate the book to the writer himself. While I was writing that dedication, however, a familiar voice spoke to me loud and clear. "Young man," it said, "I appreciate you helping to get this published, but you know good and well that this book is dedicated to Rachel." I do know that's true, because her presence permeates these pages, just as it filled the house on North Columbia Street in Milledgeville, Georgia where I had so many childhood memories. So, as Pop would have wanted, this book is dedicated to his wife of nearly sixty-one years and my grandmother, Rachel Gregory Cox.

TABLE OF CONTENTS

FOREWORD 1

PROLOGUE 8

THE LICKSKILLET DISTRICT 10

SOME EARLY MEMORIES 28

HOME AND CHURCH 41

CROSSING POLECAT MOUNTAIN 53

MY MOUNTAIN SWEET SHRUB 62

WORLD WAR II 72

   Photo Album 105

VALDOSTA 113

EMORY UNIVERSITY 121

REFLECTIONS 127

MONTEVALLO 134

MILLEDGEVILLE 137

THE FRUSTRATED FARMER 146

FAMILY AND RETIREMENT 159

   To Rachel 175

FOREWORD

Dargan Ware

My name is Dargan Ware. I spend much of my time writing. I'd like to think I'm pretty good at it. I work as a consumer protection attorney, and my function within the firm I work for is primarily the writing of briefs. I've had poems published in a number of magazines, and I've published a novel, The Legend of Colgan Toomey, that has received strong reviews.

I cannot write a foreword to this book that does it justice. My grandfather, Roy Linton Cox, Jr., may have chosen to call himself a bumpkin in the subtitle of his memoir, but he has written something that is truly universal. It is a story of rural living, of poverty, of education, of service, and, above all, of love. He has written it with humor, often of a self-deprecating bent, with warmth, and with intelligence. This book can stir your soul one moment and make you double over laughing the next. I am proud to be the one to edit it and bring it to publication, but it is my grandfather's work from beginning to end. I wish that I had been able to help him publish it before he died in 2010, but it brings me great joy to do so now.

CROSSING POLECAT MOUNTAIN

My grandfather was known to me, my siblings, and my cousins as "Pop," while his beloved Rachel was "Granny." I had never heard him refer to her as his "mountain sweet shrub" as he does herein, but his love for my grandmother was evident and palpable in everything he did. Pop and Granny radiated love and kindness. To this day, I have never seen a relationship as strong as theirs, and I doubt I ever will.

For the whole of my life, Pop and Granny lived in Milledgeville, Georgia, mostly in the big house on North Columbia Street that Pop describes in the section about Milledgeville. My family, which lived in Arkansas for most of this period, would drive in for Christmas and for a week or so preceding summer camp every year. We never went on any other vacations, except to visit them, and to my other grandmother's house in Brevard, North Carolina. Yet I loved those trips more than I would have enjoyed any fancy tourist destinations.

For me, Pop was as much a part of Milledgeville as Georgia College itself or the old capitol building. I had heard, I suppose, that he came from somewhere else, but I never put much stock in it. He and Granny were an institution. I remember being so jealous when my cousins Wesley, Leigh, and Helen King moved to Milledgeville, because they got to be close to Pop and Granny year-round.

As his life did, Pop's memoir begins in a place he calls the Lickskillet Militia District. Though it is unclear whether anyone there today would know the name Lickskillet, the road Pop mentions on the first page, Arnold Mill, is still a relatively major thoroughfare in southern Cherokee County, Georgia. These days, one finds this road by exiting Interstate 575 at Towne Lake

Parkway, which takes one into downtown Woodstock. It turns into Arnold Mill Road once you pass Main Street. Of course, no interstates or parkways were to be found when my grandfather roamed these foothills as a young man.

Pop grew up a few miles outside the small town of Woodstock. His family, lacking an automobile, would make their rare trips into town via mule-buggy, and he relates some of the amusements of these adventures in these pages. But even the town of Woodstock itself was a small, rural settlement at the time. In the framework that Pop sets up herein, it was on the same backward side of Polecat Mountain that he grew up on.

Today, Woodstock is solidly a part of suburban Atlanta. The rural, hillbilly Cherokee County of Pop's youth now has more than a quarter-million residents. The changes don't stop there. One of the schools Pop mentions, Hickory Flat, is now, at least as far its middle school is concerned, named for Pop's father's first cousin Dean Rusk. Mr. Rusk served as Secretary of State during the John F. Kennedy and Lyndon B. Johnson administrations. During the Cuban Missile Crisis, he famously stated that "we were eyeball to eyeball and the other fella just blinked." That sounds exactly like something Pop would have said.

To borrow a phrase from an Alan Jackson song, Pop was, in many ways, the quintessential "small town southern man." As is evident from these pages, Pop was a devout member of the Methodist Church and a man raised in a very traditional, conservative way. He spent most of his life in relatively rural areas, and, as is demonstrated by the section on his small farm near the end of the book, loved the land and the outdoors.

At this point, some of my readers may be imagining a politically reactionary, bigoted individual. It is true, unfortunately, that there are far too many bigots, racists, and homophobes in the South. It is just as undoubtedly true that there are far too many in every other region of the country.

My grandfather was not among them. In this book, he mentions, but takes no credit for, the integration of the Women's College of Georgia (now known as Georgia College). That was his wont. He sought little spotlight and brooked no praise. He would have said that anything he did was easy in comparison to the courage and grace shown by people who had to fight for rights he could take for granted. But he played his role with respect for everyone with whom he came into contact and a simple courage and earnestness that allowed him to always do what he felt was right. He was usually spot on about that.

This is not a political book, and Pop, at least as I knew him, was not often an overtly political man. He would have said, however, that treating every human being with dignity was not a political act. It would probably break his heart that so many of his countrymen have come to see it as one. As stated above, Roy Linton Cox, Jr. was a small-town southern man, and a proud one. He was a believing Christian and a lifelong Methodist. He lived his life in service to his country, his God, and his fellow man. In doing that, I'd argue that he was much more like Jimmy Carter than most of the southern politicians that have come along since. I think Pop would agree.

This book presents hardships and triumphs with the same wry since of humor that Pop used to approach every situation. From the hardscrabble years of the depression in the Lickskillet District to serving his country in Tezpur, India, one of the forgotten theaters of WWII, to raising a family while helping to educate a generation, this is the story of a southern life, an American life, a Christian life, and a good life. Pop has bequeathed the same to his children and grandchildren, and I will be forever thankful to him. I am also thankful that he left us this memoir and that I was able to assist in presenting it for publication.

Dargan M. Ware
October 26, 2020
Bessemer, Alabama

Wesley King

Linton Cox (Pop to me) gave himself to his community and his family. He had a profound influence on me. I am Pop's second oldest grandchild, and my parents settled down in Milledgeville when I was eight years old. From that time until I obtained a driver's license, I was fortunate to have an experience that I wouldn't change for anything – many afternoons after school was over, my sisters and I would stay with my grandparents until our mother (Pop's second child Vivian) could pick us up after she finished work. Sometimes that was at 9 PM. That gave us an incredible amount of time with Pop and Granny. Which allowed us to do what kids do – soak up knowledge and life experiences. If any part of me today is good, Pop had a lot to do with that. He was a great man. He was measured. He was funny. He was not an authoritarian, but when I needed disciplining (often), the tone of his voice did more than the back of any hand. I respected my grandfather because I could recognize even at an early age that he was good and kind.

I have vivid memories of his smile. I can still hear his thoughtful and deliberate responses to questioning. I remember playing basketball with him in his backyard. Driving out to his farm across the river. Learning about my community when he took me to his Rotary meetings. And later in my childhood I have fond memories of lunches at Cafe South with Pop and Granny. The measure of a man can be gauged in many ways. One very telling sign is how others react to his presence. Every time Pop and Granny showed up at Café South for our meat-and-three lunches, the staff and the clientele lit up. That was because they knew what I knew about my grandparents.

Pop's first grandchild is Dargan Ware. Dargan contacted me in early October 2020 to let me know he was gathering information to publish Pop's memoirs. I immediately wanted a part of this. Over the next twenty-four hours most of the members of our family were reaching out to Dargan asking what they could do to help. That is because they feel the same way I do. They feel the same way those folks at Café South felt.

Pop's legacy extends far beyond those who knew him. I have a little boy due in December 2020. My list of necessities that the child must do and experience is short. The most important thing on that list (aside from mowing the lawn by five) is spending as much time as possible with his grandparents. That necessity is directly due to the impact Roy Linton Cox Jr. left on me. It strikes me that we should all be so lucky to pass on such a legacy. I am glad he crossed Polecat Mountain.

Wesley King
October 2020
Nashville, Tennessee

PROLOGUE

THESE ARE MY MEMORIES. If some of my readers have different memories of some of the same events, that will be understandable. The minds of humans do not operate in lockstep.

I have tried to record a balanced picture of the life of a sometimes troubled country bumpkin who lived on both sides of Polecat Mountain, mentally, spiritually, and physically, and who spent a lifetime trying to "find" himself.

My search for self did not appear to me to be visible in most of my acquaintances. I did not leave home and roam or attend any rowdy youth rallies. As a matter of fact, there weren't any in or near the Lickskillet District. Anyway, Dad kept me pretty well informed as to who I was. In the cotton and corn fields, that required back aching labor, often from sun to sun, he taught me that life is not always peaches and cream. Yet the vegetable garden, the potato crops, the peach and apple trees, the watermelon and cantaloupe patches, the wheat and cane fields, all blended to make life bearable, exciting, and even enjoyable on the farm. The rough and the smooth blended at harvest time and Christmas.

My memories here are not exactly chronological in order. They just didn't come that way, although they roughly follow a sequential pattern from birth to old age. Not everything is recording here. Since I will not be offering myself for election to public service, maybe the American paparazzi will not have occasion to dig up whatever I may have left out.

My happiest days were spent with Rachel and our children, Martha Lillian, Mary Vivian, Roy Linton, III, and Evelyn Gregory. Our world was rocked when Linton died in 1990, and mine was turned upside down in 2003 when my wife of sixty-one years, Rachel, died. She was truly a love, a mountain sweet shrub. As Mark Twain has Adam say upon Eve's death, "Wheresoever she was, there was Eden."

The prospective reader may now have the impression that this is a sob story. Don't kid yourself. Read and enjoy.

THE LICKSKILLET DISTRICT
People and Attitudes

IT WASN'T AN EARTHQUAKE that caused a rumbling noise on Arnold Mill Road, Rt. 1, Woodstock, Georgia, Lickskillet Militia District of Cherokee County, on the night of December 6, 1920. It was the doctor in his horse drawn buggy rushing to traverse the six miles necessary to reach my grandparents' country home. It was about eleven P. M., my mother said, when he arrived, hitched his horse to a fence post, and delivered a twelve-pound boy destined to be Roy Linton Cox, Jr. Mother later thought it must have been an earthquake. Her account was that Dad fainted!

Now, I never bought the twelve-pound story. The doctor must have brought along his fishing scales. I was such a skinny little runt for the first quarter century of my life that I could not possibly have weighed twelve pounds at birth. I barely weighed ten times that amount when the Army Air Force got me in 1942. All our neighbors said I would never pass the physical, for the rifle would weigh more than I. But human flesh of whatever condition was needed, and I met that criterion. But I get ahead of myself here.

My grandfather, Andrew Daniel Cox, had built a large home on his four hundred acre farm, and it was there that he and my grandmother, Margaret Elizabeth (Lizzie) Rusk Cox, lived with their three children, Roy, Nellie, and Estelle. In 1919, Roy went afield, 120 miles afield, traveled by train, courted Leila Elizabeth Foster, married her in late Fall 1919, and brought her back to live in the same house until one of the renter houses he had inherited when grandfather died in 1917 could be renovated. It was to be about two years before the renovation was completed. During my first year, I was unable to help out effectively with saw, hammer and nails.

Just a few words about my Grandfather Cox will suffice. He died three years prior to my birth. Written accounts indicate that, by the time of his death at age fifty-one, he had bought and paid for four hundred acres of prime South Cherokee County, Georgia land. This allowed him to leave one hundred acres each to his wife and to his three children. Records also indicate that he was active in civic affairs, especially in education. He had been chairman of the County Board of Education and very active in the promotion of the fledgling Methodist college in northwest Cherokee County, Reinhardt. Two of his children, Roy and Nellie, graduated there in 1916. His baby daughter, Estelle, enrolled but did not return to graduate after his death. It was said, far and wide in Methodist circles, that Grandfather was a great singer.

Grandmother Lizzie was an imposing personage any way one looked at her. When she was around, everybody knew it. She was corpulent, commanding of voice, and demanding of respect. Her room in the Cox family home her daughter, Estelle, had inherited, had a frontal view through a rounded bay window. That meant she could scrutinize all the buggy and wagon traffic on the dirt road that ran close by the house. She knew who was on the courting circuit and whether each was with the same person every Saturday night. She also had a clear view of the front yards of each of her children. Breaking her apron strings was like pulling on a strand of barbed wire—thistles all the way. Dad's pliers were never sharp enough to make the final cut.

Grandmother had tremendous pride and wore it in her countenance and mannerisms. She had some basis to support this pride. She was one of eleven children born to Colonel James Edward Rusk and wife, Margaret Susanna Brooke. Colonel Rusk was of some import in the Civil War, having commanded a unit close to Rome, Georgia. He had considerable holdings in land and built a large house on it to accommodate his ever-growing family. The house still stands as of this writing [in 2004]. Grandmother used his prestige as one base for her pride. In like manner, she had married a very successful farmer who had left her in good financial condition. In addition, her husband Dan had been a community leader, achieving distinction as such. What more could a Lady need to support holding her head high? Grandmother Lizzie died in 1950, proud of her heritage.

I often wondered in my Lickskillet years whether she loved me. She never said so but when she was on her death bed, she kept calling for me. I was in Valdosta at that time and got the word that she wanted to see me. It was near registration time, and I was up to my neck in "alligators." However, I got a couple of days off and went to see her. The day I just had to get back home, she asked that I put my arm around her back and let her sit up for a while. I did that until she fell asleep for the last time, and then I eased her down on her pillow.

Did she love me? Sure she did. Some evidence of that fact had begun to surface even before her last days. Like the day she found out Dad didn't have enough money to buy me an Emory ring when I graduated. She bought me one. Now my fingers are too large at the joints to accommodate it, but I still have it. She loved me. We just didn't talk about family love in those days.

Many stories circulated about Grandmother's experiences, most of them related to her size. I was not a witness to many of them, for I was on the other side of Polecat Mountain, and the news did not scale the heights and descend to the valley below. I will repeat the two I heard most frequently, for they were confirmed by Dad, and Dad hardly confirmed anything at all that was related to his mother, and not much else either except his authority.

The privy was situated some twenty yards down the hill from the house, somewhere near the cherry tree, or maybe it was one of the peach trees. Let's just say it was near several fruit trees. In warm weather, Grandmother used the privy rather than the chamber pot that she must have found it difficult to use anyway. On one of her trips down the hill, she got nearly there but fell just short of her goal. She rolled and fumed and could not get up. Then she yelled bitterly until Uncle Harley was finally near enough to hear her and go to her rescue. When he got there and the rescue was effected, at great cost to Uncle Harley's back, Grandmother complained, "Well, Harley, I just 'wallered' like old Gus." Gus was one of the family mules.

I may have mentioned Grandmother's corpulence. I hope so, for this story is related heavily to it. Leading off the back porch was a rather steep set of wooden steps. I don't know whether termites or just plain rot had weakened those steps, but something had. Grandmother started down, and you can guess the rest. She stood on the ground with steps below her and steps above her. Pinned in, that is. All her independence captivated. Again, she had to call upon Uncle Harley to rescue her. When Uncle Harley found her, she was standing there in all her glowering glory, pleading for help. Now, he could not possibly call on his back to handle this problem. The odds were too staggering. So, he got his saw and sawed the problem away. He did so without putting any extra scratches on Grandmother's legs. A strong and resourceful man, indeed.

As my first cousin, Lanier Cook, and I grew into driving age, which was pretty young in those days, twelve for me and earlier for him as I recall, we were assigned to drive Grandmother on trips she wished to make. Once, when it was my time, she wished to go across the river to visit a relative. It so happened that her sister, Mary, who lived up the road a little piece, wanted to go with her. They loaded into the back seat of Dad's old 1930 Chevrolet and issued me the orders of the day, destination, route to follow and how fast not to drive. Each then assumed the pose of "Miss Daisy," although that movie was some decades in the future.

The route they chose offered my tempestuous soul an opportunity for mischief. The bridge across the creek was bowed sharply and I knew how breathtaking it could be to drop off on the other side. As I approached the bridge, I exceeded the designated speed limit considerably and executed my plan. Grandmother and Aunt Mary hit the top of the car and dropped back with some damage to the springs. It took them a minute to regain their composure and formulate their questions, the first being, "Linton, did you mean to do that?!! I should have answered, "define mean," but I didn't know the fine points of law in those days. Did I lie? You're damned right I did. "NO MA'AM."

My father, Roy Linton Cox, was a somber man, sometimes referred to as an Old Testament Christian. He believed in the

Father, Son and the Holy Spirit, but he lived in the Old Testament, with Abraham, Isaac and Jacob. Every night of the year, he read the Bible and prayed at length. Seldom did he call on Mother to do the praying. We all put our knees on the hard floor with our heads in our chairs—and listened. Once, Rachel yawned audibly while he was reading from Jeremiah. He had some fierce looks for her, and me, after he finally said "Amen." He had good reason to be somber. He had lost his beloved father in 1917, and on his shoulders fell the obligation to distribute his father's assets to two sisters, a mother and himself. The process was finally concluded in 1923. Why it took so long was a fact he never explained to me. Actually, he explained very little and was unhappy when questioned, so I just didn't ask.

My father also had reason for serious contemplation about his community role during the flu epidemic of 1917-19. So many of the community's male population died that he was soon the only one left with strength enough to dig graves. He told my brother, Erwin, that, in the rocky ground of the area, mainly in the cemetery at Mt. Gilead Church, he dug at least thirty graves. He must have considered his time in life to be uncertain. He was stern with me, probably loosened up a bit on Erwin, but was in any case a strict disciplinarian. He applied the switch frequently and with force, both in our private lives and in his job as a school principal. Many parents did not approve, but Dad's methods were the order of the day and he got by with applying them.

He would not abide destruction of property. My bad habit of climbing up on a chair and getting a handful of sugar from the sugar bowl brought me face to face with that fact. I dropped the top of the bowl one day and, knowing that a sentence would be imposed, took refuge at once under the house. He had extrasensory perception. He knew where I would be. When he leaned down to order me out, I didn't budge. He backed off with the statement that I would have to come out some time. When I did, I was whipped for two counts, both felonies: breaking the top of the sugar bowl, and theft by taking of about two ounces of sugar.

When there was vandalism that involved his property, he solved the mystery himself. His extrasensory perception took over. One Halloween, a group of youngsters took his buggy apart and scattered the parts all over the place, the wheels, as I recall, ended up on top of the barn. He went directly to the culprits and made them retrieve every piece of the buggy, put it back together again, and restore it to the shed it had been in. In similar fashion, he knew exactly who took two one-gallon cans of his sorghum syrup, and he gave them a piece of his mind, no syrup with it. He even knew where they had hidden it. He retrieved it himself and brought it back home!

Dad never cursed. When only slightly irritated, he would exclaim, "LAND of GOSHEN." I never learned why he mentioned that fertile piece of land when vexed. The nearest he could ever get to cursing when he mashed his thumb, bumped his head or caught a plow handle in the ribs was, "HATEFUL take it" or "DOG bite it all." When he said one or both of those, Erwin and I knew not to laugh. His fury would have landed on our backsides. The only time I ever heard him say a word that might not have been acceptable in one of his Sunday School lessons, and he didn't know I was around then, was when he was driving our cow down to Grandmother's pasture to get some greener grass than was available in ours. As the cow started across our front yard, she assumed a position and attitude that suggested her intention to mess up the freshly swept yard. He commanded her in graphic terms not to *bleep* there. She understood. She retracted the intention, went down the road a hundred yards or so, and found an acceptable place to *bleep*.

Dad never told a joke. He didn't know any jokes, and if Erwin or I even suggested we knew one, he would squelch it before it was told. Later, when I was old enough and big enough to handle him if he sought to broadside me with a slap, I would tell him one. It would take him thirty seconds or so to process it through his mind, and then he could have been heard laughing over the whole six miles to Woodstock. It was a sin, but he laughed anyway.

Only one time did I escape the rod when guilty of nefarious deeds. I was on the back porch of our house with my flip (slingshot) and a plump hen was down the hill about fifteen yards away. Now, I had never hit anything with my weapon of mass destruction before, but I took aim on that hen and hit her, smack in the head. She died instantly. Oh, God, could He save me? When Dad came in and Mother advised him of my perfidy, he doubled up in laughter. The hen was cooked and made wonderful chicken and dressing for several days. Dad did love chicken and dressing! Her un-laid eggs were pretty good too. If allowed to "set," she would have raised many fine fryers.

At the kitchen table where we ate all meals, except when the preacher or other visitors were there, it might be said that he was terroristic. We could not laugh during the meal, and even guests were required to adhere to that standard. When Mother's sister, Martha, was there on one visit, she said something funny and we both laughed—but only for about two seconds. God save the king! I will never forget his disgust when Mother was sick, and I tried to cook the hot biscuits he required for breakfast. They came out of the oven as flint rocks. He tried to bite into one and knocked his false teeth loose. He looked over at the "safe" in the kitchen where leftovers were kept and said, "Well, son, git me the cold ones." I did. Never again have I tried to cook biscuits!

If Dad and I were estranged to some degree in early life, we were reconciled in his later years. He dearly loved Reinhardt College and wanted one more trip to his Alma Mater. I took him. Much of the little town of Waleska, the site of the College, was as he had known it in 1914-16. Most of the same buildings stood on campus. He wanted while there to visit Briar Patch cemetery where several of his favorite professors are buried. We went there and he spent much time reading the inscriptions on their monuments. On another trip, he wanted to have some time in the Mt. Gilead Church cemetery. I took him there and, since he could not walk well, I took him by the hand and led him through like a small child. He went to the graves of his parents, stood and stared for several minutes, then to those of his sisters and to Estelle's husband, Harley Cook. Finally, he said, "Son I'm ready to go home." Tears came in the corners of his eyes. That was a Sunday. The next day, he died at eleven a.m. on the front porch of the house he had built in 1925. His death was in August, 1982. He was at home. When Mother died in 1994, she was in a Milledgeville nursing home. I took her back to his side and placed markers as he had prescribed them.

He lived in awe of death and the hereafter. He planned to the last letter what should be done when he died. He should be buried with his thick glasses on. Otherwise, he would not be recognizable. He picked out exactly what clothes he would be buried in. Erwin and I, noticing that he had let his "Sunday clothes" get bare, once took him to town and bought him a new suit. He decided that would be his burial suit, and more than two decades later, it was. He met his Master in a nice suit, for he had not worn it much. Since he did not specify shoes, I suppose he entered the pearly gates barefooted.

Did I say he never told a joke? I think I did. Nobody else told one around him either, especially not at any gathering that met in the church building. But facetious I could get away with! Since there were so many Rusks buried in the Mount Gilead Methodist Church cemetery, the Rusk family reunion was held on church grounds for many years—dinner on the grounds and a business session in the church building in the afternoon. Well, one year they made the mistake of electing me President of the Rusk Family Memorial Association, Inc. The reunion that summer was in July. If Hell is any hotter than that summer was, we'll all melt and run out our ears when we get there. In the afternoon, I was presiding at the business session. The crowd was large, and we didn't have enough funeral home fans to go around. Everybody had sweated through every piece of clothing they had on. It seemed we might soon need caskets rather than fans.

I was of the mind to tell a joke, come Hell or hot water. I was standing near the spot where Sister Zeigler had once described Hell in heated detail. So, I said to the Association assembled: "You know this heat reminds me of the family traveling West during the gold rush. They reached Hot Springs, Arkansas late in the afternoon. They unhitched the mules and began preparations for spending the night there. The father took a bucket to the springs for to fetch some cool water, and was shocked to see steam arising from the water. He rushed back toward the wagon shouting, "Hitch the mules to the wagon boys. We ain't a half mile from Hell."

From shocked looks to painful grins to loud laughter took about ten seconds. Bellies shook that had been deprived of a good shaking for several decades. Even Dad laughed, in spite of the fact that his eldest son had clear committed a grievous sin by telling a joke in the Church building.

Dad was a good man. Above all he loved God and the Church and the Bible. He didn't curse, he didn't drink booze, he didn't smoke, he didn't chew, he didn't sniff snuff, he didn't tell jokes. It was said that he didn't have much fun.

Leila Elizabeth Foster Cox ("Miss Leila"), in addition to being recognized as one of the best cooks around, was also known as a woman of deepest religious faith. She built a little rock altar in the woods behind our house, and in dry weather spent hours there communicating with God. She taught children at Sunday School for fifty years, always seeking fundamentalist literature for distribution to her pupils. Her literature sometimes became a matter of controversy because it was not "modern" enough. She believed the "second coming" was imminent and often sang as she worked, "I will arise and go to Jesus, He will embrace me in His arms. In the arms of my dear Savior, oh there are ten thousand charms."

Mother was always afraid she would have no souls to her credit when she met her Master, and since she believed He would appear presently, this sometimes bore heavily on her mind. She often would sing "Will there be any stars in my crown, when at evening the sun goeth down." At every revival, when altar call time came, she would move across the Church exhorting individual "sinners" to go to the altar, pour out their hearts to God, and be saved. This was especially significant, adding gloom to the already generally depressing atmosphere spawned by the Great Depression. Mother was not the only one engaging in these tearful pleas. Others of the faithful did the same thing, creating a steam bath of emotion.

There was definitely a downside to these revivals. Some who were adjudged sinners because they had not yet been seen at the altar remained stone faced, while some went to the altar every summer and could not "come through." Mother believed that God had promised her that each of her sons would be a minister of the gospel. Neither of those promises materialized. She believed community morals were her responsibility and sometimes was hurt because some of those she sought to counsel did not wish to be counseled.

Later, after I was in the Army Air Corps and banished to India near the lair of the Naga Head Hunters, Rachel ran headlong into the community mind set, and I do mean "set." In concrete. Belief was that a wife should live with the husband's parents while he was away. Rachel was disappointed to have to leave her widowed Mother, but she was going to do it for my sake! I knew nothing of this *bleep*, but thank God for my mother-in-law, Carrie Peeples Gregory. She had met my family, the whole family, including Grandmother Lizzie, at a summer picnic near Chatsworth. She exercised her mountain authority in a decisive manner. "You will stay right here with me," she told Rachel. That was final; there was no appeal procedure.

Then, Lickskillet "feel terrible" screws were put on Rachel to spend every weekend with Mother and Dad. She couldn't do that, of course, so tsk, tsk went the community. She must be running around up in Chatsworth, etc. Rachel did spend as many weekends down there as possible, but then her dress style came into question. She had bought new slacks and took them on one trip. "Oh honey," mother said, "Women just don't wear pants around here." Luckily, Rachel had taken one dress that met the qualifications. I should have given her a book stating Lickskillet Regulations, but they were not codified, just solidified. The pants prohibition was, of course, in effect to keep women from appearing to be manly. Per St. Paul the Apostle. But the keepers of the gospel were inconsistent. A woman couldn't hide her legs with pants, but when dresses went up to the knees, wagging tongues were heard for miles. The uproar was even louder when some brave ladies moved their hemlines upward. Oh, Lord! One somewhat profane keeper of propriety approached one of the escalating sinners and asked her when she would have her surgery, reasoning that if her dress inched much higher, she would be forced to have her *bleep* moved up.

When decades later, Rachel was far enough away from these things to reveal them unto me, I went about the house uttering all the obscenities I had ever heard, including the new ones I had picked up in the Army.

Yet, I must conclude by saying that Mother was a good mother.

Five other houses existed within a half-mile radius of Dad's dream house. Four were usually occupied by tenant farmers, the other by a widow whose husband, Samuel McWhorter, had been killed by lightning several years earlier and who had left her and their three children more than a hundred acres of land adjacent to Grandfather's western border. Mr. McWhorter and my grandfather had served together on the Cherokee County Board of Education. Lightning struck quite often in a little abandoned cemetery near where he was killed. We often expressed the opinion that someone pretty wicked must have been buried there. His widow taught school in Woodstock and rented quarters there during winter months. I always anticipated eagerly their return home for the summer months, for of her three children, one was a son who was one of my parentally approved playmates. I later grieved deeply when he was shot to pieces in the "Battle of the Bulge" in Europe.

Tenant farmers in the other four houses were often destitute and we helped them all we could, to a point! They were always required to put a portion of their farm produce in our barn and crib. One man could not understand the concept of land ownership. He argued that if he and his sons worked in the hot sun to grow various crops, they should keep it all. Dad and Grandmother gave him a short course in the sanctity of ownership, and he divvied up. Poor man. Nobody seemed to know exactly from whence he came; some said Arkansas, others Alabama. He and his sons had serious conflicts. The oldest chased him around the house with a hammer. Another reported that "Pa killed a man in Alabama." But he and his large family had many good points. He was a master blacksmith. They worked hard, and the wife and mother could whomp up a bodaciously delicious country meal.

Down through the woods back of our house, two hundred yards or so below our outhouse, lived a tragic family. The father was addicted to "moonshine" and was violent when under the influence. On Saturday afternoons we could hear loud shouting and cursing. Once the father threw a fire shovel and cut through his young son's upper lip. Later, he was somewhere in Atlanta and couldn't be found when that son died of diphtheria.

Comic relief did come now and then. A couple with three children moved into the easternmost renter house. Now, they would have dances in their house! That was a sin. They would pay "Uncle John" and his band of black musicians one bottle of 3.2 beer each to play for the dances. The alcohol was also a sin. Tongues wagged about the utter debauchery that must be associated with such wanton sinfulness. To top it all, as my brother pointed out recently, the father streaked. He got up at five o'clock every morning, went outside, and ran around the house naked. God would surely exact revenge. I'm not going to record here what actually happened to the three children. Tore my insides, until I could look at it from the other side of Polecat Mountain. (Explanation later).

Certainly, other social activities existed in the community. Some of them are tellable. Others must die in the caverns of the ages. Now, in the community lived a spinster, her age at the top levels of middle age, assuming she would live to be a hundred five, otherwise at the middle level of old age. She was slender, prim, some said a prune-faced lady. Her name was Ella Belle Larson (names changed to protect everybody). At the same time, Grandmother had a brother, Taylor, who lived down toward Atlanta, and he had an eye for Miss Ella Belle. When he would visit Grandmother, he would call Miss Ella Belle on the community party line, that was the same as a radio broadcasting station.

Occasionally on such visits, he would stop by to see his nephew, Roy, who, as previously stated, was my Dad. On one such visit, he brought his fiddle and asked Dad whether he might call Miss E on the party line. Of course, permission was granted. Uncle T. greeted Miss E with some gentle comments, then stated that he wished to play her a fiddle tune over the line. He let the receiver hang down, sat with his instrument under it, and played at length. I don't remember what tune he played, probably something like "Turkey in the Straw." I never learned what Miss E's response was when he returned to voice transmission. In any case, she wasn't interested in him.

Instead, in due time, she married Bob Horton, a man a decade older than she. Before long, she announced to the ladies, under her breath as required, that she was pregnant. Through the ladies who still communicated with their husbands, the word spread through the community like wildfire. Reckon Old Bob could do something like that?! If he did, his effort ended in tragedy. The next announcement that came through the pipeline was that Miss E. had aborted. Oh, my!

As stated earlier, it was into the Cox home that I was born. I don't remember living there, I was just told that I did and that the "going" was pretty rough with so many folks in the house. Mother felt that she was considered a second-class member of the family, a peasant in a class of lords and ladies. Her parents, Lovick Pierce Smith Foster and his wife, Henrietta Matilda Blanton were tenant farmers of less than modest means. In other words, they didn't have *bleep* in physical possessions. But they had what counted: love, and faith in the Author of love. Since I was not precocious enough to evaluate the Cox house atmosphere for myself, I will leave that at that.

Some of my Foster family materials have been lost in various moves from residence to residence, but enough remains, mostly in Mother's writings, to support some facts and observations. Mother was the second of eight children born to Lovick and Henrietta Foster. One child, Mary, died at age five. All others lived to adult ages and produced offspring.

I'll get my grandparents on the scene by saying a few words about their parents. My paternal great grandfather was John Thomas Foster, who was a confederate soldier, a sergeant in the Infantry. He married Martha Trussell. He was Sheriff of Upson County, Georgia, 1881-1893. My maternal great grandfather was Benjamin Gregory Blanton who married Leila Frances Marshall. Benjamin died early, and Leila moved to Texas where she married a Mr. Garrett. The Garretts soon moved back to Georgia and then back to Texas. I am not sure of the dates. The last recorded migration to Texas was in 1895. From that combination came Lovick Pierce

CROSSING POLECAT MOUNTAIN

Smith Foster and Henrietta Matilda Blanton, my grandparents. She called him "Lovey." He called her "Hennie."

If the Fosters or Blantons ever owned land, I don't know about it. I once asked Mother whether her parents ever owned land. She replied in the negative, that they were always tenant farmers. Whether my great grandparents ever owned land, prior or subsequent to the Civil War is also unknown to me. Anyway, my "Little" Grandma, so-called because she never weighed more than 100 pounds, and my Grandfather, so-called because he was, were aristocrats in Christian Love. It might be said here that my "Little" Grandmother and my corpulent Grandmother saw each other no more than a half dozen times! All things considered, that was probably propitious. They are both deceased.

My Grandparents lived in counties in the vicinity of Columbus, Georgia. Grandfather died in a house near Shiloh, Georgia, that I think is in Harris County, and Grandmother died in Pine Mountain Valley, Georgia. I think that is in the same county. Pine Mountain Valley is a long way from Pine Log Mountain where my Sweet Mountain Shrub agreed to become my mate forever. We were on different sides of Polecat Mountain, which was my great continental divide. But I digress.

Soon our house down on the river was ready for my parents and I to move in. It was a pre-Civil War log house with 12-inch hewn boards covering the logs. A fireplace in the "front room" was framed by a mantel and the visible bricks were whitewashed. The white was severely stained by amber when some of the neighbors visited.

One man could and would sit ten feet away, tuck his thumb under his chin, stick a finger across one corner of his mouth and spray the whole fireplace, leaving a streak across the floor that verified his aim. A kitchen and eating area were joined to the back of the house. I did not know all this, of course, until I was told later. My first memory of life there is of a doctor coming to our front porch and lancing a boil under my arm. I was held for the operation on the lap of my favorite uncle. That helped.

SOME EARLY MEMORIES

THOSE BOILS CONTINUED TO PLAGUE ME well into my adult years, the last one hitting me in the nose in the early 1980s. They were sharply painful and lasted three or four days. When I was old enough to ask questions about such matters, I was told the cause of the boils was "bad blood!" Bad blood?! How come my blood was bad? Did those that happened when I was a baby occur because of my original sin? There was a large scar on my left wrist. I inquired as to the cause. Bad case of erysipelas, I was told. The doctor had to be called, they said. Thought they were going to lose me. Lose me?! That was fuel for several days of contemplation.

I also remember an incident in that house that was very painful for me. I decided to show my parents a thing or two. They demanded that I not get too close to the fire. In a fit of anger, I backed swiftly onto the hearth and sat down on the firedogs. I had gone to hell backwards! Phoenix-like, I arose from my own ashes. Who could forget a thing like that?!

I was a puny child. My frail frame bothered many. I wouldn't drink my milk, so Aunt Nellie would walk down the road to our house and pay me a penny per glass to drink it. Up into my early teens, I would faint for no apparent reason, just fall in my tracks. I don't think any doctor ever knew of that symptom. If any did, nothing was done. I learned that the best way to get my balance back was to crawl to the coldest spot on the wooden floor and put my face on it until my equilibrium was restored. In the early thirties, malaria hit me for three years. I was never really healthy until I crossed Polecat Mountain (explanation coming). If we had been noble folks with titles in those pre-Polecat days, mine would have been His Puniness.

My poor health as a child led to a number of dire statements about my tonsils. Every time I got a sore throat, I was sure I was dying of diphtheria. Both country doctors we used expressed deep concern about the condition of my throat in general and my tonsils in particular. Finally, one of them said to Dad in my presence, "Roy, if you don't have this boy's tonsils taken out, he will never amount to anything." So now, dear reader, you know why! Dad and I would never agree to having them excised. One kid we knew about had bled to death as a result of that surgery, and I was scared. I'm sure Dad was too, or he would have ordered me to get on the table.

The condition of my throat and tonsils improved on the other side of Polecat Mountain.

My closing remarks about Dad must take a different approach. He had lost his beloved father who was only fifty-one at his death. Although Dad had survived the flu-generated holocaust, he had dug the graves of many who did not. He had gone through the rigors of distributing his father's property. Those matters must have weighed heavily on his outlook. But there was more.

CROSSING POLECAT MOUNTAIN

The Lickskillet District was infested with copperhead snakes. Dad had nearly died at the behest of one of them. It is said that most snakes are not aggressive. The copperhead is. I have seen them crawl almost at lightning speed toward persons who had not attacked them. They are vicious terrorists. That aside, Dad saw many of them in his life and felt that was an ill omen. During his last years, they continued to pester him. On two separate occasions, a copperhead crawled up on the porch near where he was sitting in his rocker and almost paralyzed him with fear. On each occasion, a passing neighbor killed his tormentor.

Now, I ask myself in figurative sackcloth whether I've been fair to him. I strongly suspect that under similar circumstances, I, too, would have been a somber man. I'll never know. I killed two rattlesnakes on land we owned, but only because I am prejudiced against poisonous snakes. They scare me *bleepless,* as demonstrated by the morning I had picked a gallon of blackberries, only to fling my berries to the wind when I noted that right in front of my eyes was a long reptile that had also decided to avail itself of the luscious fruit. This was in the Lickskillet District. I cried and ran up the hill to the safety of home.

Our next house, after the one down by the river, was another renter house at the top of the hill from that first one. It was also a log cabin structure, with logs planked over. We were getting closer to the site where Dad planned to build our permanent residence. My first recollection of that third house is of Mother's heavenly cooking—biscuits, cornbread, vegetables, ham, chicken, beef, pies—I must stop here, or I shall perish at the very thought. I used my psychology on Mother. When she refused to give me another cookie I would inquire as to her love for me. When she affirmed that, of course, she loved me, I would ask her to prove it by giving me another cookie. It was widely believed that I was a mischievous brat! That was a sin and resulted in several charges being lodged against me.

In that house, we were directly across the road from the site of the family home that was yet to be built. An old barn stood there, a barn that was later used for our livestock. It had a loft for feed storage and a crib downstairs for corn. One use of that corn was meal for our cornbread. Uncle Harley had a mill and converted the corn into meal, taking $1/8^{th}$ as payment before the corn was crushed.

When the family house was about to be constructed, Uncle Harley brought his Fordson tractor and pulled the barn across the road to the front of the house we were living in at that time. Dad built a kiln near the site of the house and cured the lumber that had been sawed from trees on his and Grandmother's land. He departed from his raisin' a bit to buy tongue and groove lumber for flooring, walls, and ceiling. He hired a carpenter and the two of them built the house. I think Dad said he paid the carpenter a dollar per day!

There was a kitchen, a dining room, two bedrooms and a "front" room that was used as a living room. A wide hallway ran down the middle. At the back of the hallway, a dining area was defined, to be separated off by French doors. The doors were never purchased. Wide porches were at front and back. Before the back porch was built, a well was dug under one end of it and tiled all the way up to the porch. A windlass was installed on the porch. From that well we drew our water for all purposes. It was the coldest and best freestone water that ever graced an aquifer, and the coldest I have ever bathed in on Saturday night. To this day, the memory of it makes me abhor the sulfurous water of coastal areas.

Dad's dream house, complete with smokehouse and outhouse, was completed early in 1925, and we moved in. Our outhouse was down beyond the smokehouse, in the edge of the woods. It was a handsome structure, even had two holes, but I never knew of an occasion when there was more than one person in there at the same time. In emergencies, one might hide in the woods with the chiggers. The outhouse was equipped with Sears Roebuck catalogs and a supply of corn cobs in the corner in case all catalogs had been crumpled and in their final resting place. We heard that one neighbor lady who was about to enter the hospital told her husband to be sure to carry a supply of cobs along, for "she knowed in reason they wouldn't have none there."

The community, the Lickskillet Militia District of Cherokee County, was quite rural, bucolic, and pastoral. Six miles separated the community from Woodstock and three miles from Chadwick's store, depending on the way one was traveling. Woodstock had weenies and ice cream, a drug store and other good things not available at Chadwick's. However, Chadwick's held its own with adequate farm supplies, a cordial atmosphere and nail kegs to sit on while discussing news of the community, state, nation and world. A Saturday afternoon at either place was a glorious treat.

What kind of folks were we the people who lived in that community? Salt of the earth? Maybe. Depends on the composition of the salt. Define salt. We were above all judgmental. We were born into that kind of atmosphere and knew no other way. Apparently, we read the Bible to say, "Be sure I will find out your sins and when I find them out, God help you." That's not the way it's written. That's the way we lived it. That was the community norm and, I must add, there were exceptions, as there are to any norm. If our brother offended us, we wouldn't forgive him, and *vice-versa*. We believed that Jesus would forgive us but be damned if we would forgive each other. Strange interpretation!

We were often contentious, always religious by rote, gossipy. Hear, hear!! I must not be too hard on us. The salt of the earth was in us. We helped each other at harvesting time, at hog-killing time, at any time of need. We were kind to each other in times of illness and death. If one family got down on its luck, the rest of us pitched in to help them get back on their feet. One family would promise work time, three days, four days, whatever time was needed. Another would promise food, another help with laundry needs. We brought each other back to independent living, by loving, by caring in the name of God.

Some words were never said in the Lickskillet District. For instance, breast. That word might cause thoughts of something ugly and sinful. So, women didn't have breasts as far as I knew. They had some kind of bulges on their chests, but kids were not supposed to know what they were. Except for the possibility that I was breast fed (I was never informed about that and didn't dare ask), I never saw one until much later. I saw W. H. get R. T. behind the jacketed stove in our classroom and rub her chest vigorously, but I assumed that R. T. was in some sort of pain and needed a rub down. Similarly, there was that ugly word, pregnant. A swelling stomach indicated a lady was "in a family way," and even that was said in hushed tones. When the baby came, either the stork or the doctor brought it. Actually, the word pregnant is not a word to be ashamed to say at all. It is pregnant with words. A great test of one's vocabulary can be taken at the reader's leisure. Just look at the words imbedded within it, words like gnat, peg, pant, pet, grant, get, ran, and many more.

Body parts and bodily functions just were never to be mentioned. To do so would get a child a terrifying beating. So, we stayed pure and undefiled. But guess what. I found out in the Army that certain words previously thought to be vulgar did not mean anything like what they were supposed to mean. The "F" word was not just a verb, rather an adjective to be spliced in before every noun.

Here, I shift gears to describe some of my experiences as I came into consciousness of what was going on in the community. My first memory after moving into the new house is of summer 1925. Records were set for drought and heat. The little stream called Little River dried up to a trickle about three inches wide. Crops dried up in the field. It was a time of gloom reflected in the faces of Dad and Mother.

Gloom had already taken over in our household when Dad, while shucking corn in our crib, was bitten by a copperhead snake. He was a man of retribution and doggedly raked corn until he found and slew the offending reptile. The exercise necessary to do that increased his blood flow, something his system didn't need at that crucial time. By the time he got Aunt Nellie to take him to the doctor, a mile away, he was already sickening from the poison. The doctor was not skilled in the treatment of serpent poisoning and simply poured a quantity of carbolic acid in the wound. That could have been the accepted remedy of the day. I don't know.

At any rate, Dad became very sick. I remember asking mother whether my Daddy was going to die. She answered that she didn't know, that she was doing all she could to get him well. The gloom was thick enough to roll up in sheets. Neighbors came in with long faces, shook their heads and left. The Holly Springs Circuit minister came in and prayed, put his hand on my head, but left without comforting words. Hope was locked up with a Schlage dead bolt lock and we were on the wrong side of the door. There was a drought of the spirit.

Maybe "touched by an angel" is the right term here. Dad began gradually to gain strength. I sat on the front porch with him as he propped his wounded foot up as high as possible to ease the pain. The flesh had fallen off his ankle and the healing process was long and painful. I brought him cool water when he wanted it. Occasionally, he wanted biscuits, butter and jelly, and I would bring all the necessary ingredients to him. Somehow, there was just enough rain to spare the cotton in that summer of drought. As we sat on the front porch, Dad and I could see Mother across the road picking cotton. She had a straw hat under which she placed large oak leaves as cooling agents. That summer, she single-handedly picked four bales of cotton of approximately five hundred pounds each. Neighbors hauled the raw cotton to the gin for processing, then later hauled the bales to Woodstock for sale. There was never any profit in it. Cotton was no longer King Cotton. It was a peasant, subsisting on depleted soil. Yet Dad stuck to it as a "money crop." The merchant took the money.

Toward the end of the summer, Dad's ankle had begun to heal. He decided it was well enough for him to take his place in the sorghum field and help harvest that crop. Fundamental gloom again. His decision had disastrous consequences. He came home with his ankle bleeding and needing attention he didn't seek. The fall was long and the healing again slow.

Somehow, I've never gotten over the feeling that when God told the serpent it would get its head bruised by man, He issued a mandate to me to bruise every snake head I see! Why in Heaven's name would Noah take two copperheads, two rattlesnakes and two cobras on the Ark? Surely, he could have substituted six less vicious creatures. Snakes serve one purpose for me. They keep me scared *bleepless*.

As the mid-twenties ascended toward the end, my experiences expanded and became more memorable. School days were determined by agricultural needs. We were needed at home until cotton was harvested, and sometimes fall attendance had to be interrupted to allow for fodder pulling, corn harvesting, wheat thrashing, hay cutting and storing, placing potatoes in "hills" for winter use, and similar activities. Winter attendance was usually uninterrupted, but in early spring school was "out" until fall. Teachers were paid a pittance for a maximum of seven months a year and sometimes paid in script. I can't remember whether the script was ever redeemed.

Our school, Modesto or Hickory Flat, was either one mile away or five miles away, depending on where Dad was principal. Transportation was sometimes walking, but most of the time, it was riding in a mule drawn buggy. In really cold weather, Dad had a heavy lap robe that was over his lap and over all of me as I sat down just behind the dashboard. Heat was provided by a heated rock wrapped in another blanket. The rock was heated at the fireplace. Direction of the wind determined whether Dad got any invigorating fresh air on those trips. When warm days came our conveyance was a one-horse wagon. That allowed us to take along some neighboring kids who ordinarily walked. The seats were terribly uncomfortable for those with bony bottoms. We forded a creek on the way and often stopped for the mule to drink. On one such occasion, I stood up to ease the pain in my bony parts and the mule jumped forward, pitching me in the creek where a rocky bed awaited me. I ought to have stayed seated. Dad took me on to school, wet.

Episodes in the Life of a Bumpkin

My first day at school was an embarrassing disaster. That was at Hickory Flat. This class was called the Primer in those days. Immediately, my seatmate took it upon himself to tell me the facts of life, in gory detail. He named each body part, not in biological terms, but in gutter language and indicated the function of each. My playmates had been so limited by my parents that I had never heard of such information. I could hardly wait to get home that afternoon to inform Dad and Mother where W. H. told me I came from. That was a bad mistake. I got a spanking for telling them, and Dad gave W. H. a beating the next day for telling me. W. H. was furious and no more was my seatmate! He said he would never tell me anything again. I considered this threatened deprivation fortuitous, since we both got our asses beat over his first revelation. When I received similar information in the future, I just pondered it in my heart!!

Being the Principal's son had its drawbacks. He made life harder on me than on the rest. But, generally, school days were pleasant. We played ball of a kind during recess, attended "chapel" every day, and studied mathematics, spelling, English, and civics. In the ninth grade, I played on the basketball team at Hickory Flat and we competed with other area schools. The jockey strap my parents got for me was too large and I lost it while playing against the Avery school. Just one of life's embarrassing moments. The coach was kind and took me off the court for the rest of the game.

"Academic" subjects took precedence in the classroom. If we didn't learn the multiplication tables, we didn't get promoted. If we couldn't spell, our grades suffered. If we couldn't look at a sentence and identify the subject, predicate, adjective, adverb, and such other parts as existed in the sentence, we were held up for ridicule among our fellow students. I'm very glad our instruction was rigid. Skills learned in the early grades were all important in the building of a successful life and career. If one has not parsed a long sentence correctly, one has not lived. If one does not know instantaneously that 8 x 9 = 72, one gets a calculator. If one cannot spell Mississippi, one is not alone.

Teachers sometimes played tricks on students. When I was in fifth grade, a party was set up for students at Modesto School. It was an evening affair where the girls brought cakes, and the boys bid on those cakes to see who would get to eat with the prettiest girls. The Great Depression had started, and the bids were low, so some pretty girls and their cakes went at bargain prices! I did not participate in that contest, for I was afraid of girls! Ice would have frozen my vocal cords if I had tried to converse with one of them. There was a guessing contest where participants tried to guess the number of seeds in a lemon and the one who named the correct number would get a cake. I guessed fourteen seeds. It was announced that I had won, and I was summoned forward. The cake was wrapped in beautiful paper that I peeled away eagerly. When I opened the cake-sized box, a small bar of soap was in it. I was angry enough to kill the teacher who made me the butt of such a joke, but Dad wouldn't let me. He thought it hilariously funny. As a matter of fact, I suspected him of planning the hoax.

Meantime, back at what might have been called Flint Rock Estates, we eagerly awaited spring and the warmth necessary for Dad and Mother to approve going bare footed. When they made the momentous decision, we ran quickly into the yard and promptly knocked off a toenail or two on those flint rocks. By the end of the summer our feet were so tough nothing could hurt them except a stone bruise, which required puncturing the bruised area, often with a safety pin or needle. Then we again donned a pair of shoes for fall and winter. Sometimes, we had to wear the same pair at least two years.

The Great Depression years, approximately 1929-1942, caused gloom all over the land. Then is when I learned the true meaning of "Son, we just don't have any money." I would try to hire out to pick cotton at ten cents a hundred pounds, sometimes got a job, then heard the above statement when collection time came. What a crushing blow. Dad had a job, but it paid only seven months a year at fifty dollars a month. His farming operations didn't bring in any cash, but, of course, allowed us to grow corn, wheat, vegetables to can, potatoes, and other food items. At least we could eat and share with our less fortunate neighbors. We had meat from hogs and chickens, never much beef but plenty of fresh milk—unpasteurized!

During those years, President Roosevelt and Congress set up a number of programs to ease the pain of poverty and to boost the economy. One of them was the Civilian Conservation Corps. In that program, young men could enroll in camps and do various conservation and beautification projects. They were paid a small stipend, and a dollar per month went home to the parents. They built parks and did numerous community enhancement projects. Every dollar helped, and, meager as the stipend was, it was an effort that helped many families bear the gloom.

In the camps, each enrollee had his assigned duty, keeping the area clean and neat, being chief cook or other kitchen duties, and providing heat in the winter months. I've forgotten what the fuel was, but I think it was coal. There was not much worry in those days about polluting the air or the great outdoors. There was a rule about those camp responsibilities. One didn't complain as to the quality of job one's camp mate was doing, and this applied specifically to the quality of food. If a complaint was lodged against the cook, a job nobody wanted, the complainer had to take over the job. This was a two-edged sword. It might freeze one forever in the cook's position. It was reported that a resourceful cook, who had never been challenged, cooked up a surefire plan to get rid of the odious duty. He would cook horse manure balls instead of sausage for breakfast. Someone would surely complain about that. The perfidious act took place. The first young man to bite in jumped up and yelled, "That's not sausage, that's horse *bleep*... but I like it!"

Another such "New Deal" program was the Works Progress Administration, or in some quarters called the We Piddle Around Program. Adults were paid to engage in a variety of public projects and given a small hourly wage for their efforts. The workers could often be seen leaning on their shovels or picks or whatever tool they were using. The story circulated that several men had died from leaning on their shovel handles so long that they rotted and crumbled—the shovel handles, not the workers.

A surplus food distribution program was initiated at some point during the Great Depression. A neighbor lady across the branch from us went up to Canton and got her ration, which included a head of lettuce. She told the neighborhood that she cooked that stuff all morning and it still was not fit to eat. Was there mirth amidst the gloom? Sometimes.

HOME AND CHURCH

WHEN COLD WEATHER CAME, hog killings were a great social event. The whole neighborhood pitched in to help scald the brute, scrape off the hair, and cut it into appropriate pieces. Hams and sausage were prepared for curing, the hams usually cured with salt in a large wooden box, the sausage either hung from rafters in the smoke house, or canned. Ample sage, peppers and other spices had been dried and ground. Lard was rendered in the wash pot. That was my job and God help me if I let the cracklings burn in the bottom of the pot. Those morsels had to be saved for crackling bread. "Mammy's little baby loved crackling bread," only this one didn't! It was common practice for the family that had a hog killing to distribute a "mess" of pork to each of those who helped in the processing. It all evened out by the end of the season. Nobody lost anything by being generous.

Our meat supply was augmented by rabbits. I had up to eight rabbit boxes each year set out on Dad's farm and would visit those boxes every morning on cold mornings. Sometimes we got a rabbit. Hunters would often tear my boxes up, for there weren't enough rabbits to go around. Once we got a polecat, and we didn't eat it. I shot it with my Dad's twelve-gauge shotgun because it messed up my overalls. Took a week to boil the odor out!

When our mule or cow died, we cried all day. Where on earth would we get the money to replace the animal? Then, suddenly a neighbor would appear at the door with many crumpled ones, a few fives and a whole lot of change (butter and egg money) all of which would add up to enough to buy another animal. The same approach prevailed all over the community. When one uncle's barn that had hay for winter feeding and corn stored in it was burned down by a disgruntled neighbor (never prosecuted but generally believed), a new and better barn was soon erected at no cost for labor. Some trees were donated for lumber also.

Speaking of barns, it was my duty in early spring to clean out the stables and haul the manure to the fields. I had never heard of Hercules at that time, but I found out later that he had a similar task at the Augean stables. At least he had running water.

By the time I was ten, a mule and I were plowing all day in our cotton and corn patches, but never had I plowed a horse before being assigned to plow out the middles in Mr. W's corn patch. Both Mr. and Mrs. W. had been ill all summer with malaria and needed some help fast. I told Dad I would take my own mule for the task, but he said "No." Mr. W. wanted his horse to get the exercise! Well, I bolted a wide scrape on the plowstock (a sweep we called it) to take care of my assigned responsibility. I finally found a singletree and attached it to the plow stock. Then came the task of getting the horse harnessed and hitched to the singletree.

That final task was a whopper. The horse, stabled all summer, didn't care to be harnessed. He danced around all over the lot, defying my every attempt to get his bridle on and the bit in his mouth. I had to bribe him with hay, finally tricked him to get all of his paraphernalia on. A wild stallion would not have been harder to handle. He didn't know the meaning of Whoa! I think he interpreted that as "woe." I had to bring the plow to him to get his harness hooked to the single tree. He wouldn't go to it! Finally, mission accomplished, I directed him out of the gate and got him between two corn rows. He didn't understand his role in the operation. All he wanted to do was eat the leaves off the corn stalks. I went back to the barn and found a muzzle. That was the ultimate insult to him. He slung his head about as if he had been stung by hornets.

At last, I got him in forward motion—at about forty miles per hour! He thought he was Pegasus and set out to prove it. The standard method of slowing a spirited animal down was to raise the handles of the plow and thrust the point deep into the ground. He hadn't heard of that method. You can't do that anyway with a wide scrape in thick crab grass, especially not at forty miles per hour. As I jerked on one plow line or the other, depending on which row of corn he was requiring me to plow up, I had to turn one handle loose. And when we were turning at the end to select another middle to mess up, God preserve us both. When we finished that day in Mr. W.'s corn patch, it didn't look the same as when we started. A streak of grass here had been smeared over by the scrape, another streak there smiled as if nothing had happened. In many places, the corn itself had been trampled. Mr. W. had lost some corn, I had lost my temper and almost all the religion Sister Zeigler had bestowed on me. The horse had lost nothing.

So, that was the first day I had ever plowed a horse—and the last. The next day Dad let me take our mule down there and straighten out the mess.

CROSSING POLECAT MOUNTAIN

Also, by ten years of age, I was able to take care of one end of a crosscut saw with Dad on the other. On a cold, frosty morning we would go at daybreak to one of the forests on the Cox land, select a couple of trees for firewood, build a fire nearby and get to work. I enjoyed that. By the end of the day we would have the trees cut in blocks, split and ready to haul home. Usually, the hauling would have to wait until the next day. We were, in modern terminology, pooped! It was a good pooped.

My job at home was to keep wood in the house stacked near the fireplace and cook stove. We burned oak in the fireplace and pine in the cook stove. By extension, my job was to bank the fire in the kitchen fireplace at night, and get up early to stoke the coals with more wood, so that when Dad went in for his breakfast, he would not get his bare feet cold. My bare feet got really cold, for there was no heat at all in the house when the coals were banked under ashes. About five o'clock in the morning, Dad would yell to me "Get up son and start the fire." If I pretended not to hear and snoozed a couple of minutes, the second yell would be, "Son, are you going to build the fire, or do I have to come in there after you?" At that question, my feet hit the floor. He never had to "come in there after me." He would start the fire somewhere else, more painful than my frozen feet.

I learned the art of splitting the stove wood into manageable sizes to fit into the fire chamber on the cook stove. This process involved imbedding one blade of a double bit axe into a stump or large block of wood, leaving the other blade up. A large piece of pine wood, already sawed to stove wood length, was then raised high and brought down with force on the blade. The end result of several such blows was that a neat pile of stove wood would be generated, and a half-day of such maneuvering would produce enough for a month or more for the cooking of three meals a day. Since work gloves were hard to come by, a side effect would be picking splinters out of my hands at night.

Here, I digress to tell of the birth of my brother, my only sibling. Erwin Pafford Cox was born August 16, 1926. I suppose I knew Mother had gained in size, but I don't remember. Such things were never discussed. I had no idea where babies came from until W. H. told me on the first day of school. All I remember is that one morning early I was sent away to play with a neighbor boy. The boy had sisters, but I was to maintain a respectful distance from them. When I came back home late that afternoon, there he was, a ten-pound specimen of humanity in bed with Mother. The doctor brought him, I was told. I was to wait until school opened to find out where he really came from!

He and I developed a close relationship. There was a young oak tree in the front yard, and for the next ten years, we spent many hours under the shade of that tree. In the early years of that period, I "minded" him while Dad and Mother worked in the fields. I was his guardian and protector. Then, for his first Christmas, good old Jolly St. Nicholas brought us a little red coaster wagon, and on warm days I pulled Erwin all over creation in it. One day the only community vagrant came by and told me he was going to "steal" my little brother. When Mother came out of the cotton patch that night, I asked her whether it might be possible for me to kill somebody, drag the victim off into the swamp, and not get caught! She didn't think well of the idea at all. That would be a sin. Later, when a cousin threw sand in my little brother's eyes, I beat the offender up. Dad beat me up for beating him up. I thought that was a sin.

Then one day when Erwin was three or four, I was engaged in the wood splitting function, about fifty yards from the house. I drew the double bit axe up and back to imbed it in a stump. The absolutely unthinkable thing happened. My little brother had wandered down to where I was and was standing directly behind me. When I heard the thud and turned around to see blood streaming from his forehead, I went berserk, running about the yard screaming "I've killed my little brother, I've killed my little brother." Dad, hearing the commotion, rushed to bring him to the house. The telephone party line was activated. Aunt Estelle was called, and she immediately activated Grandmother.

When Grandmother didn't arrive at once, I ran to the middle of the road to see whether she was on the way. She was—shuffling along as fast as her corpulent self could shuffle. When she arrived and assessed the damage, she looked in the fireplace, grabbed a handful of soot and rubbed it into the wound. Erwin was rushed to Coker hospital in Canton, where the doctors spent more than two hours removing the soot and, it was said, uttering a few profane remarks during the process. But Grandmother had used the old-time remedy for stopping bleeding. She had come when needed with nothing in mind other than saving Erwin. The hospital doctors did the rest. More than a dozen stitches had been required to close the wound.

When the entourage arrived back home, I was assured I had not killed my little brother.

I used the word "rote" earlier to describe religion in our community. The elders of whatever denomination one might be in all had the same approaches to God. They used the same phrases and the same intonations over and over. Those were the phrases they had learned from their parents and ministers and they from theirs from the foundation of the world. I never heard a young person pray in church. We were not asked to do so. I guess because we had not memorized the proper approaches to the Throne. Even in my youth, I felt that God must get awfully tired of hearing nothing new.

In church services, the men sat on one side of the pulpit area and the women on the other. God forbid that husband and wife should show any affection for each other on God's Holy Property, inside the building or on the grounds. That would be "ugly." All was to be long-faced and somber. If young children, brought into the Church for "Preaching' misbehaved, they were taken out by the mother, whose licks on behinds sore from sitting on hard benches could be heard. The loud squalls of the offender told all that the treatment was taking effect, and when the kid was brought back in, he or she misbehaved no more. In the minds of the elders, the parent was a good one, bringing up her children in the nurture of the Lord.

Revivals were everywhere during the summer, usually two weeks in length. We attended at least five of those revivals to show community good will, and to be on the safe side anyway. Sister Leila Cox was called upon to pray in every one of those "meetings" except the Holy Rollers. I don't think the Holy Roller people knew that frontier Methodism had customs of emotionalism very similar to theirs. Most Methodists didn't know it either! I didn't until I was in the third year of college. Revivalists sought to "convert" sinners and bring them into the fellowship of the redeemed and into true discipleship. This was, of course, a noble aim springing from the very heart of the Church Universal. But the nature of the emotional appeals got many kids to the altar who knew nothing of what they were doing. They were seeking the approbation of their parents and the friends of their parents. A shining face arising from the altar was the facilitator for glowing countenances among the elders, often loud shouting.

The shouting always aggravated Grandmother, a Presbyterian turned Methodist only because the Presbyterian Church was six miles away in Woodstock. Besides, she couldn't climb in a one-horse or two-horse wagon. In one meeting, somebody let out a shrill shout, "Praise God!" Grandmother turned around, stared at her and said, "Well, scare a body to death!" When she didn't like a sermon, she would pleat her handkerchief all the way through her ordeal, then give the preacher hell on his way out the door, pointing out his errors—her duty, don't you know.

My "conversion" occurred one hot summer when Sister Zeigler from Miami was invited to conduct a two-week revival in our little Church, Mt. Gilead Methodist. She had the reputation of bringing the sheaves down the aisle, and I soon found out why. She told terrible tales of sinners who had rejected the call and had died Hell bound. It was awfully hard on my skinny tail to sit still on a bench and listen to her hour-long harangues, followed by an altar call of at least thirty minutes. One evening, the mourners' bench was full, and they mourned mightily. I held my seat, on a cushion my parents had allowed me to bring, and was all set to resist the call. Sister Zeigler was flapping her arms, shouting, trying to look everyone straight in the eye, and finally she spotted my cushion, I guess. With a mighty bang on the lectern, a blow that would have broken the average hand, she yelled, "Some of you folks out there are riding a cushioned seat to Hell!" Oh Lord! I was on my way. For days, I had fears of meeting Satan face to face. I may have, but, if so, he didn't recognize me.

In regular Sunday services, once a month, sometimes in the afternoon, sometimes in the morning, it was time for Mr. E. to get his daily nap. He would snore in perfect time with a song, with loud crescendos. Always when the preacher would come down hard with a bang on the pulpit, Mr. E. would awaken for a moment, nod his head vigorously, and promptly resume his snoring. Parents would assume an amused look, but children were required to maintain a sour countenance. Now, Mr. E. had fathered thirteen or fourteen children with the same woman. He and Mrs. E. were worn out, and Mr. E. deserved that rest on Sunday after having worked all week in the fields. Mrs. E. usually stayed home and cooked for her flock.

In addition to established churches where revivals were held, there were tent meetings, open air meetings, brush arbor meetings, and camp meetings. The Marietta Camp had several cabins around it. The faithful owned or rented those cabins and each summer would come for a week or two of revival and religious recreation. Evangelists would preach and exhort sinners to righteousness and the faithful to renewal. Sometimes, even a fervent evangelist would need to return to the fold. I remember one handsome man of the cloth found comfort with a wife while the husband was out of his cabin. Trouble was, the husband did not stay out long enough! Next day, the evangelist wept before the congregation and obtained the husband's forgiveness. There was never any word about whether the wife was accorded equal absolution.

The entire community was saturated with thoughts of the second coming. I often wondered, even then, what the elders did with Matthew 25:13 or Luke 17: 20-21, or all the times Jesus said, "The Kingdom of Heaven is at hand" or all of the above. But it has seldom ever been nice to question the elders, as perfectly portrayed in Bach's *Jonathan Livingston Seagull.* Believe Jesus or John of Patmos?

When children went out to play in the morning, they were told to be good, for Jesus might come today. Mother was sure Jesus was on His way every day, would be there just any moment. This had a profound effect on Erwin, my brother. He created quite a stir in the community when my Uncle from Harris County drove up in our front yard in his new Ford roadster and set down on his air horn. My brother and a first cousin were playing out of sight of the house and when the horn tore the air, Erwin proclaimed "Jesus has come!" They sought out the cousin's father and gave him the startling news. That Uncle had heard the horn too. He took the boys down the road to our yard, showed them the horn, and said to the roadster owner, "You ain't Jesus!"

Our pastors on the eight-point Holly Springs circuit, of which our Mt. Gilead was a member, were paid practically nothing. They had a parsonage in Holly Springs and that was about all. They visited parishioners often to enjoy a meal and fellowship. Usually, the pastors were granted "first table" and ate up all the good pieces of fried chicken before my brother and I could gain admission to the table. But we got good food, the vegetables we needed to stay healthy. We had little resentment, for the presence of the preacher in our house was a holy event. We were required to address him as brother and his wife, if any, as sister. On one pastoral visit, there was a humorous exchange between Mother and the pastor. She had served all the butter we had, and the pastor was given first choice. Mother said, "Brother Pilgrim, please don't be afraid of that little bit of butter." He replied, "Sister Cox, I would not be afraid of three times that much butter." He is now deceased.

Our pastors never left our home empty-handed. If we had fresh vegetables, we would give them a "mess" of corn, several tomatoes, okra, beans—whatever we had. In winter they took with them canned vegetables, sausage, just whatever we had. One pastor let it be known that a couple from another church had given him a milk cow and that he was keeping this source of fresh milk on the parsonage front lawn. Trouble there was that the critter had eaten all the grass and now had nothing to eat. We were feeding corn shucks to our milk cow, so we offered him a wagon load of shucks. He returned the next day with a borrowed wagon and got his shucks. Erwin and I helped him load the shucks and were hard put to hold in our mirth when he bumped his bald head on the roof of the shed the shucks were in, then raised his eyes to Heaven as if to say, "Why me, Lord?" He is now deceased.

Were our morals so bad that we needed all that emphasis on religion? Some thought so. But in retrospect, it seems to me they were about the same as they were elsewhere. A sip of Lum Crow toddy at night was a delicacy that tempted many. It was a sin, but a good and accepted sin. As reported earlier, some boys trashed Dad's buggy. That was just as bad. A man over in another community, with roots in ours, fathered an illegitimate child, and another fathered three, not by the same woman, of course. The latter, when asked whether he planned to marry the lady, said "no" but he sure enjoyed the process. That was absolute apostasy. A divorced man a few miles away, who married a lassie half his age in our community, was widely rumored to have murdered his first wife. But, after all, she was his. A sin? Yes, but she just might have been a fishwife, maybe even a piranha. A few razor skirmishes here and there hardly deserve mention. Those were to be expected, as were wife beatings on Saturday afternoon. Occasionally, a wife was so unruly that she had to be beaten in the middle of the week! Otherwise, the area was rather Christian.

Blurred time elapsed. One year, I was out of school for almost the full year due to severe complications from measles and some other childhood ailments. I had to repeat that year, either the sixth or seventh grade. The early nineteen thirties were quite hard years on my health. I had malaria three years running. We lived near a swamp and the mosquitoes had a picnic. Nearly everyone in the community had malaria. Quinine was the only prescription and it didn't seem to retard the chills and fever in the least. Uncle Harley, Aunt Estelle's husband, always cradled our wheat while I went along behind him and tied it up in bundles. Dad could not see well enough to do those tedious jobs. I saw Uncle Harley cradle part way across the field and when a chill came on, he lay down, shook until the chill stopped, then went back to his task. There was no time to stop work just to pet a malaria attack.

CROSSING POLECAT MOUNTAIN

I PROMISED EARLIER to explain my title "Crossing Polecat Mountain." Here it is!

In her historical novel, *A Little Leaven,* Cherokee Publishing Company, 1984, Frances E. Adair relates the story of a group of Virginia residents, "who left Virginia to settle in the Salacoa Valley of Cherokee County, Georgia." The time of this migration was just prior to the beginning of the Civil War. When the group arrived at the little village of Etowah, the leaders found that they must be ferried across the Etowah River. Obviously, that would take a good bit of time. Inquiry was made as to whether they could make it to the Salacoa Valley by sundown. A local citizen replied, "You can't hope to, stranger. That stretch across Polecat Mountain is a long dangerous drive."

In a different sense, that stretch was still a dangerous drive a century later.

In 1935, I entered the ninth grade at Hickory Flat School where Dad was principal at that time. During that school year, much discussion occurred as to where I would go for the remaining two years of high school, the tenth and eleventh grades. There were only eleven grades in those years. I could have driven twenty-four miles per day in the 1930 Chevrolet, twelve to Canton and twelve back, to Cherokee County High, but Dad was unhappy with that thought. He really wanted me to go to his alma mater, Reinhardt in Waleska, Georgia where a high school was still attached to the Junior College. He decided that was far and away the best choice.

In August, 1936, Mother packed my clothes in the same trunk Dad had used in his Reinhardt years. We loaded the trunk into the old 1930 Chevrolet and struck out across Polecat Mountain into Waleska. The Boys' Dormitory had plenty of space, and I was assigned to a corner room. My roommate was a Cuban boy, Juan Francisco Carbinelly Garcia from Santiago de Cuba. I tried to get him to teach me Spanish, but all he taught me were words and phrases I couldn't use later! On one of my very few weekend trips home, I took him with me. He and I both were subjected to harsh stares because his skin was a couple shades darker than mine. I wasn't supposed to be getting that kind of education at Reinhardt!

Dad talked to the President, Dr. Bratton, and got me a job washing dishes in the College dining room. Dr. Bratton drove his Hudson Terraplane all over the campus in second gear. On Sunday mornings, he would pull it close to the steps of the Boy's Dorm and spring out to uncover any student who had hoped to sleep in and miss the long sermon we were all expected to hear. A long cigar graced his lips. He would leave it on the windowsill of his outer office, which tempted some students to do unspeakable things to it. But I digress, again.

I settled in and started studying to please the folks back home. But by the end of the first week, I was thoroughly dejected and ready to get the hell out of there. A college student had taken my light bulb out, inserted a piece of cardboard into the socket, and screwed the bulb back in. I didn't know anything about electric lights, for all of my studying at home had been by kerosene lamp. As darkness was approaching, my tormentor came to the room door and noted that the light was out. He explained that at Reinhardt each student was required to furnish his own light bulbs and that he just happened to have an extra which he would sell me for fifteen cents. I barely had that much money, but I found enough to buy the bulb.

Then he had a good laugh and told me he had been kidding. He folded in derisive laughter and offered me my money back. I was so angry I would have loved to kick him hard in the groin, but he was too tall. I refused to take the money back, explaining that where I came from a deal was a deal. He left the room and never came back. Other means of harassment were associated with initiation into the Pierce Literary Society. Dad had been a member of that Society when he was a student there. That initiation tore my only white shirt and subjected me to an unspeakable encounter with a certain item related to feminine hygiene. I knew the item existed but had never seen one. Furthermore, while I was away getting initiated, some bum put an item related to male contraception, filled with water, in my bed. I was thoroughly disgusted and worried. I didn't want to live in an atmosphere like that.

As my second weekend approached, I wrote the folks at home to come and get me, that I would plow the rest of my life before I would live in a pig pen like Reinhardt, that I was coming home. Nobody came. Mother wrote me a short note. "Dad says, 'No, you're not.'" I was mad at the whole damned world. I had been rejected and abandoned, and that at the tender age of fifteen.

CROSSING POLECAT MOUNTAIN

Although home was only twenty-five miles away, it was across Polecat Mountain—it was a whole world away. There was no balm in Gilead for me and, as time elapsed, I didn't try to remedy that. I had survived physically that long dangerous stretch. Now it was time to pursue its broader meaning.

I now count this "abandonment" as being high on the list of the most thoughtful things Dad ever did for me. He sent me to Reinhardt as something he could do for me that he could never accomplish in the Lickskillet District. He took the dangerous step, knowing that I might think for myself, that I might develop, or assimilate into my convictions, different religious views from those he had inherited from his forebears. This was a thought Mother abhorred. She saw as sinister any questioning of traditional interpretations and traditions of the past. Dad took the gamble. I wish I could tell him now how much I appreciate that.

Reinhardt had some excellent teachers, and I was able, even in my high school years, to get sound instruction in mathematics, grammar, English literature, Latin, French, and history that I don't believe I would have gotten in the county high school. I came to love my studies and to see ever more clearly that "there was something else out there." In the meantime, social events were few. The College students had "rules off" occasionally, which meant that they could date according to the whims of the President's wife, if a chaperone could be found. Couples were forbidden to touch each other. Many seemed to find crannies in which to hide for a moment, but not for long! I wasn't dating, so it didn't matter to me what was going on or coming off.

One night, as I walked Rachel back to her dormitory from a program of some kind in the college auditorium, we were holding hands. The only route to her dorm ran by the President's home, but we thought that if he were anywhere around, his lights would be on. All was dark. As we got about to mid-point of his front porch, a booming voice yelled, "Boy, drop that girl's hand and see me in my office tomorrow morning." Oh, good grief! I nearly dropped dead. He would send me home, and I would be disgraced forever. Rachel assured me he would do no such thing. I don't know how she knew, but next morning when I reported to headquarters, he was gone to Nashville and the subject never arose again.

Miss G. was one of the best, yet toughest, teachers at Reinhardt. Her field was English, and she demanded perfection in both grammar and literature. When she gave an assignment in composition, every word must be used correctly, every comma and period must be placed exactly as she had explained the rules. When she asked for a paper on a certain author and his or her works, the student had best be prepared to defend what he or she wrote in that paper. For the serious student, she made grammar fun and literature inspiring.

For others she was a bear, and someone wrote that on the board one day before class. When she came for class and saw written there "Miss G. is a bear," her face turned several colors at once, and then—and then she walked up and down each row, stopped at each desk, and required the student to look her in the eye. Her stern stare was more damaging than Mammy Yokum's double whammy. To each student, it seemed that she would stand in that pose for eternity. Suddenly the question would come, "Do you think I am a bear?" The universal answer was "NO Ma'am." One of the possibilities was that a fellow professor, our French teacher, wrote the accusation on the board. He had written a paper for a student, and the student had turned in the work as his own. The grade was "C". This made Dr. S., the French teacher, furious. He said to our class, "I feel like going down there to that Miss G. and telling her that I wrote that paper." There was enmity between them. They are now deceased.

Miss G. exercised authority far beyond her teaching responsibilities. She was the chaperone who was reported to have had an unfortunate love affair. The way we changed class periods at Reinhardt was that a student would leave class at the proper time and ring a bell up and down the hallways. One year, I had the bell ringer job. Well, I had better not leave Miss G.'s class even thirty seconds early. In fact, I could not. She would direct me to keep my seat, for she still had x-number of seconds left. In other words, my watch must be synchronized with hers! I gave up that job the next year.

I still benefit from her teaching, and for that I honor her memory.

My main extracurricular activity was participation in the Pierce Literary Society. In two of the four years I was at Reinhardt, I was on the championship debate team. I don't remember which two it was. The first time, the Pierce side lost, and it was my fault. I forgot my memorized speech! My parents had crossed Polecat Mountain to see me triumph, and I had fizzled. I felt like an egg-sucking dog and lower than a snake's belly. I stopped by a little store on the way back to the dorm and bought me a King Edward cigar. That thing made me so sick that I haven't smoked a cigar since. The next time I was on the team, we won. I could reason as the debate ensued and didn't have to memorize a speech. One lives and one learns with some pretty hard knocks along the way.

If all of the happenings during my four years at Reinhardt were recorded, several large volumes would begin to tell the story. My mind won't separate now the year each episode occurred. But here are some happenings on the Reinhardt scene.

Episodes in the Life of a Bumpkin

We invented streaking at Reinhardt. That occurred sometime during the late nineteen thirties. Only folks like Lady Godiva had done it before and she did it across the sea, not in the socially pure atmosphere of the United States of America. In one of the cold winters I was there, I had a classmate named Jason Bowman (name changed to protect everybody). Now, Jason was from Texas. His father was a friend of Reinhardt's President Bratton. Everything in Texas was bigger. Now, Jason decided to organize a streaking society. He got no takers amongst other students, so he decided he would do it himself. In Texas it was not a sin. Jason's price was that the rest of us would raise five dollars for him. I kicked in a dime. Other more generous contributions boosted my investment to his required stipend. He selected the date and time, midnight being his selected hour. When the time was at hand, he stripped down to the attire God gave him, danced a jig as his feet hit the outside steps, and sped away. Indeed, it seemed everything was bigger in Texas.

His account of the round trip went like this: "I ran through the middle of town, past the unmanned police station, past the post office and down by the girls' dorm where I heard no female screaming voices, either going or coming back. I ran on down by the doctor's house and past the last store in town. Then I ran back. Nobody stirred." Well, at midnight on a cold winter night when there had been no advertisement of the coming attraction, is it any wonder nobody stirred? He had bamboozled us, had our five dollars, and he suffered no worse than cold feet and perhaps another part or two.

Some comedy/tragedy events at Reinhardt probably deserve mentioning. In one, Jason played the leading role. A virus invaded the campus and a mighty explosion took place, students tossing and blasting with gastro-esophogeal disease dotting the landscape. I don't know how both Rachel and I escaped, but we did, and the dining hall was getting the blame for encouraging the virus to strike. Whatever, it was an awful mess.

Anyway, a group of male students had obtained permission that Friday afternoon to walk to Canton to see a movie. They had to cross Polecat Mountain to get there. Now, Jason was a member of that hiking expedition and before he got over Polecat he was assaulted by a violent episode of diarrhea. Finally, he was lying on the shoulder of the road in terrible pain. According to his story, he passed out and was finally picked up by someone who took him to Coker's Hospital in Canton. The "Good Samaritan" did not promise to come back or to pay Jason's bill! He said that when he woke up the next morning he felt that he must have crossed the bar. He had read Alfred Lord Tennyson. But, he continued, when a Nurse in white walked in he knew that if he had crossed, he had made it into Heaven. All he had crossed was Polecat Mountain, going the wrong way. His first remark to the nurse was, "Confidentially, Nurse, I think I *bleeped*." Her quick response was, "Confidentially, Jason, I KNOW you *bleeped."* Jason is now deceased.

Some of the students at Reinhardt were "farm boys." They lived off campus and helped take care of the college's farm operations. One of their duties was to milk the cows and transport the milk to the college dining room. Sometimes, a portion of the milk would go astray and wind up in the boy's dorm. It would so happen that one or more students would have cocoa and sugar in their rooms. All of the ingredients would somehow appear in the boiler room, as would a utensil. The rest is obvious. Every student who liked hot chocolate just happened to have a cup in his room. Now, it seems amazing that so many circumstantial factors converged in the same place at the same time.

The same type of situation sometimes happened when a student would accidentally fall on a college chicken. The fall would kill the chicken, and, of course, it must be processed and eaten before it spoiled. We must have been living right to merit such blessings, though according to Lickskillet standards, I felt there must be a sin in there somewhere.

I graduated from Reinhardt High School in 1938.

MY MOUNTAIN SWEET SHRUB
And then I met Rachel

THE LOVELIEST PERSON I have ever known was my wife for sixty years, eleven and one half months. Rachel Gregory Cox died April 28, 2003. May 16, 2003 would have marked our sixty-first anniversary.

We met at Reinhardt College in 1938, near the opening of the fall quarter. Rachel was a farm girl from Murray County, Georgia. Her family farm was on Holly Creek in plain view of majestic Fort Mountain. I was a farm boy from south Cherokee County, Georgia. Our farm was located on Little River in view of a hill, which rose a few feet on the other side of the river. Both of us were members of small Methodist Churches. Her church was larger than mine. She was much more sophisticated than I.

Low profits from farming in the nineteen thirties made it necessary that we work to pay expenses. Rachel was a waitress in the college dining room, and there I worked as a table cleaner and dishwasher. I was a backward bumpkin, having had nothing to do with girls and having no desire to change that. So many possible events associated with dating were sinful, according to social standards of my boyhood community, that I had decided to let dating alone. In Rachel's community, there were fewer activities associated with sin.

It turned out that the dining hall waitresses were plotting. They sought some way to remedy my social deficiency. Finally, they decided to hold an election amongst themselves to elect an ambassador to ask me for a date. Rachel was elected and dispatched to the kitchen. I was washing and slinging dishes like mad and heard this voice say, "Would you have a date with me this afternoon?" She said I stammered and stuttered and uttered all sorts of incoherent phrases and finally came out with an affirmative answer. All I remember is that when I looked up and saw that beautiful girl with the absolutely stunning smile, all my previous instructions as to the likely sins of dating were repealed. So, we really met over a tub of dirty dishwater. "Touched by an angel"?

It was Sunday, and we had both been in Methodist services that morning, so we went to Baptist services that afternoon. I later supposed that the preacher took a text and preached, but neither of us could ever remember what he preached about or, indeed, whether he preached at all. If there is such a thing as love at first sight, that was it.

We dated during the Fall of 1938 at such times as the administration permitted it, always under the watchful eye of a sour teacher, who, it was said, had had an unfortunate love affair. Try as we might, couples could not escape that piercing gaze. When spring picnic time came around, there were a few more possibilities for semi-privacy. The picnic was always held at Pine Log Mountain, four miles west of the campus. So, in spring 1939, we selected our lunches from the dining hall and took a hayride to the mountain, steep side. We scaled the mountain almost with a single bound and found a rock behind which to eat our sandwiches and discuss international relations between Murray and Cherokee Counties. We thought we were hidden from the roving professors who sought to document the picnic. Fat chance.

It was our French professor who observed our intellectual discourse, so we found out the next day. He was a jolly fellow, completely out of tune with the top administration. He bounded into class spouting French and pointed to me as the one who should put his words into English. By the time he finished, he had forced me to describe the day from the perspective of Rachel and me! The class was in uproar, so much so that other professors were looking in to see what the ruckus was about. It was on Pine Log Mountain that we were "engaged to be married." We made bold to seal it with a kiss, magic! If I had known then how politics works, I would have, before proposing, asked Rachel to "define marriage."

We went on dates as often as "rules off" was approved. One cold, icy weekend we were permitted to date around the clock, except at night, of course. Who could do anything nefarious on an iceberg? Anyway, a board about a foot wide spanned a chasm, called a ditch, connecting the campus to the town of Waleska. Well of course the *bleep bleeped* board was slick as owl *bleep* and Rachel hit the bottom of the chasm on her *bleep*. Nothing was broken. I got down in the ditch and pushed while someone else pulled. It was up one foot and back two or three. Of course, that was O. K. with me. No reference to the biblical ox in the ditch is appropriate here. This was on Saturday, not Sunday, or was Saturday the right sabbath? It gets so complicated.

Lovers are fairly resourceful in finding ways to avoid supervision. There were some very fine muscadine vines down in the Reinhardt farm valley. Every fall, when the delicious members of the grape family ripened, a few couples would wander down that way for the ostensible purpose of gathering muscadines. That was a yearly unchaperoned outing, for in the reasoning of the administration, who could do anything scandalous down there among the ants and chiggers? The ingenuity of lovers is sometimes overlooked. Anyway, we never brought back any fruit to share. As a matter of fact, we never found many muscadines. I'm not even sure we looked for any.

In summers, I visited Rachel as often as possible, which was as often as I could get the Cox family car. That wasn't easy, inasmuch as my family felt I should wait an indefinite period of time to get "serious." Get serious? That's what I had been all my life. I might get drafted and leave a poor pregnant wife. She would have a child and the father might be killed in action, a sobering but not a definitive thought with me. I did have sense enough to know there are ways to prevent pregnancy.

One summer, I taught her to drive her 1937 Ford car. We had many narrow escapes; I suppose because of my poor teaching skills. Perhaps I did not prepare my lectures thoroughly enough. I knew the ins and outs of driving, but I had not had any "how to" education courses. In one of my lessons, I instructed her to turn right at the next intersection. She turned left—there was no road to the left. Not much damage occurred to the car. Cars were made of metal in those days. Speaking of cars and ingenuity, one summer, Rachel got me a job up in Murray County, but it didn't last long. It involved the use of a car and Dad sent me word to bring his back home!

CROSSING POLECAT MOUNTAIN

The job required me to measure land under President Roosevelt's "Triple A" farm program. The measurements sometimes showed that farmers had over-planted their cotton patches and they had to plow up some. In my short tenure, two farmers had threatened to shoot my *bleep* off if I measured their land. Each had a shotgun in the crook of his arm. I didn't measure their land, for I wanted to keep my *bleep*. The sheriff and my boss had to do their measurements. One old mountaineer showed me his still and offered me a dipper full of mash. I declined on the basis that I was on duty! One old mountaineer brought his single-barrel shotgun to town, and when told he couldn't have a loaded gun in the city limits, he proved he could by killing one policeman and wounding four others without receiving a single scratch. Maybe it was fortuitous that Dad called his car back home.

When we graduated from Reinhardt in 1940, Rachel returned to Murray County to teach in the public schools, and I enrolled at Emory University. Emory continued with accelerated pace to open new vistas for me. I majored in history and took mostly history courses at the rate of fifteen quarter hours per quarter, but occasionally a course in another field was thrown in. There was Dr. Dewey's course in Fine Arts 101. I was lost. Nobody had ever told me on either side of Polecat Mountain that people with names like Gainesborough and Van Gogh and Michaelangelo and Da Vinci had lived and done things. Nobody had ever said anything to me about a flying buttress. If they had, I would have put my hat on. Nobody had ever mentioned a frieze to me. If they had, I would have gotten my coat. I was flunking the course until an assistant to Dr. Dewey told me that Dr. Dewey thought I should "explode my points." I got the message! I went to the library, checked out several art books, and learned all the big words and names I could absorb. I made a B in the course.

Then there was the political science course under Mr. Stubbs. I nearly flunked it too, for I could not remember the difference between *and* and &. I did better in the fascinating course, History of the Far East, under Dr. Arva Floyd. If I could, I would take that same course again under the same Professor Floyd. Our history courses were made even more interesting through the International Relations organization and through visiting dignitaries such as Prince Hubertus zu Loewenstein. I may not be able to spell it now, but I remember his eye-opening lectures. Geographically, Emory was on the same side of Polecat Mountain as Lickskillet, but, as did Reinhardt, Emory provided a new beginning, different, but each a new start. God knows, it was exhilarating.

There was a downside to my great Emory awakening. My criminal record began there. I was arrested by a Dekalb county policeman. The occasion of my arrest was the death of Rachel's father, Seth Cleveland Gregory in 1941. No! I didn't kill him! I liked him. He had called me "a young whippersnapper," which I was. I had been to Chatsworth a few days before and was with the family when he died. Now it was time to go back to his funeral. To get there on time, I had to catch the earliest trolley in Emory Village and ride to the Atlanta Greyhound bus station downtown. The day before, I had secured a fellow student to substitute for me in the Emory Cafeteria, so I was able to get to the trolley stop twenty minutes or so early. Darkness still covered the landscape, except for a streetlamp near the stop.

I had been at the stop about five minutes when a car came out of nowhere and headed straight for me. The headlights blinded me, and I stepped back into the underbrush to try to hide from certain disaster. The car came to a screeching stop and two uniformed policemen emerged with pistols drawn. Of course, true to form, I was scared *bleepless*. The four arms of the law (two each) extracted me from the bushes with some force. It seemed to me at that time that my funeral would immediately follow Mr. Gregory's. Miranda was missing in those days. No rights whatsoever were mentioned to me. I was a detainee, *incognito.*

They pushed me into the police car and began their interrogation. "Why did you run?" they inquired. I wanted to ask them what they expected with their bright lights shining in my eyes and their car roaring toward me, but my mule-plowing sense told me to let my answers be short and respectful. Otherwise, I reasoned, I would be plowing that mule again, forever on the wrong side of Polecat Mountain. I explained in great detail why I was at the trolley stop. They accused me of making up the story as I went.

The time neared for my ride to arrive. If I missed that, I would miss being by Rachel's side in her dark moments. I explained faster and harder that I was not the thief they happened to be looking for. I didn't have much identification in my wallet, but I showed them what I had. As my trolley rumbled closer, the *gendarmes* dismissed me just in time, with a stern warning that if I turned out to be the thief they were looking for they would find me and make it tough on me. I didn't have to ask them to define tough. I had one more hurdle to face. The trolley conductor had seen the law release me. As I reached the door of his conveyance, he looked me over good before opening up. Finally, he let me in and at that point I was his only passenger. He eyed me all the way to the next stop where he picked up more passengers. He was then safe from my thieving heart.

Such was the beginning of my criminal career, and my journey to a funeral that might well have been my own.

Episodes in the Life of a Bumpkin

Three weeks before I graduated from Emory, Rachel's school was "out." I rented a long limousine, with driver, to take me up to Chatsworth, Georgia to claim my Mountain Sweet Shrub. We were married in the Methodist parsonage in Chatsworth, May 16, 1942. Rachel's sister and brother-in-law, Edna Earle and Dawn Coffey, transported us from dear Mama Gregory's home to the parsonage. Other witnesses were Rachel's brothers, Henley and Jathan. Reverend G. C. Burtz, Pastor of the Chatsworth Methodist Church, and his wife were awaiting us, ready to "marry off" the last unmarried sister of the five Gregory girls.

It was a simple wedding, no fancy clothing to describe, no tuxedos rented, no bachelor party the night before, no bridal shower, just a plain simple joining together of two kindred souls. We both wore our best "Sunday clothes" and that was it. The minister probably pronounced us man and wife. That was the order of the day. But we were never anything other than husband and wife. We were so glad to be together, there was no thought of one dominating the other. I put the forty-dollar ring Rachel had bought for herself on her finger and we said our vows. She wore that ring for sixty-one years. I look on it now with great reverence. I gave Reverend Burtz three dollars, borrowed from Rachel! That three-dollar wedding held us together for sixty-one years. Bragging? You bet I am!

Soon the limousine driver pulled up to transport us back to Atlanta, where we both had jobs in the Emory cafeteria the next morning. The limousine had been decorated just for us. The artists who designed the decorations had even painted a large greyhound on each side and assembled an entourage to escort us. Luxury beyond imagination!

We caught the trolley from the limousine station in mid-Atlanta to Emory, where we had taken a one-room "apartment" in a house on the corner of Clifton and North Decatur Roads, belonging to a very inquisitive old soul who had a habit of opening doors without knocking. The "apartment" had no tub or shower, only a commode and sink, and the owner had a passkey. I think that house is now the Baptist Student Union. One of my classmates soon moved. Then we got a larger room in the same house that had a bathtub and that was better than the galvanized wash tubs we had used at home.

In the trolleys of that day, the framework of seats was made of wood and there were many carvings on the back of those seats. On some of the seats, there were carvings about which Rachel was totally uneducated. I had been educated about those things in elementary school. She looked at one four-letter word, raised her voice above the whine and rumblings of the trolley, and asked me what it meant. Oh Lord! Had crossing Polecat Mountain prepared me for such an emergency? All eyes around us turned on me. Everybody was awaiting my answer with great anticipation. After what seemed to me to be a millennium, I was, I suppose, "touched by an angel." I got my answer from somewhere. I said, "I really don't know. But I have a dictionary at our room and will look it up when we get there." There were looks of disappointment all around!

My friends had organized a party for us that night, so we finally got to bed in the wee hours of the morning. We slept only three hours before having to go to work in the cafeteria. I still owed Rachel a honeymoon when she died over sixty years later, April 28, 2003. We really didn't need a honeymoon. Just being together was honeymoon enough, and we often affirmed that fact. I also owed her forty dollars for her wedding ring, but that's another story.

Episodes in the Life of a Bumpkin

I entered Emory Graduate School that summer, but our stay there was soon cut short by my draft notice. Manpower in our armed forces was dwindling and had to be reinforced with new recruits. Rachel went back to Chatsworth to teach, and I went to Fort McPherson to be inducted. We did not see each other again for three years except for a brief train trip she made to Chanute Field, Illinois, where I was in training to assist pilots in learning instrument flying. I couldn't get much time off.

WORLD WAR II

SOON I WAS IN INDIA, near the "Hump," where some of the pilots had been sent with no instrument training. Rachel often remarked that for long periods of time she didn't know whether I was alive or dead. I wrote as often as I was permitted to write. Those were bleak years. Monsoons were as a whole world weeping at once. Earthquakes were as a thousand wakeup shakes in the morning. Human misery of the "natives" was as a whole nation discarded. Loss of our crews in the "Hump" was utter despair.

There was inadequate communication among the various elements of the war effort. For instance, the folks "back home" were asked to save their fruit cocktail and send it to the boys overseas. So, here came a heavy box of fruit cocktail all the way to northeastern India. Rachel had done without so I could have that delicacy. The trouble was that we were having fruit cocktail morning, noon and night and were tired of it. I wrote Rachel and gently asked her to keep it for herself, that we really had an adequate amount in India.

Finally, in August 1945, President Truman made the controversial decision to drop "The Bomb." Whatever that did to the world, it gave millions of forlorn soldiers more time with loved ones back home. For Rachel and me, it was 58 more years, and for those 58 years, I thank God Almighty. I re-entered graduate school at Emory in January 1946 and Rachel, pregnant with our first daughter, came to join me in a war surplus trailer in "Trailer Village" on the Emory Campus. Rachel gave birth to Lillian on July 10, and I received my Master of Arts degree in mid-August 1946.

In the March 1995 issue of *Ex-CBI Roundup*, Dwight O. King, Editor, is published an article I wrote titled "Around the World Through Tezpur." I draw heavily from that article in describing my Army Air Force experiences in WW II. I spent most of my time overseas in Tezpur, India at the 1327 Army Air Force Base Unit.

I arrived there in summer 1943 and barely escaped westward in August 1945, after President Truman mercifully spared the world further duration of WW II. I wrote my parents and Rachel from Camp Luna, near Las Vegas, New Mexico on April 12, 1943:

> "The 22nd Ferry Group is on alert to ship at any time. Our First Lieutenant told us this afternoon that there is much water between us and our destination—no furloughs, no application for OCS, no transfer possible. I did want to come home before I went across, but I guess I was just unfortunate along that line."

On August 22, 1945, I wrote them: "I'm in Casablanca waiting for a ride the rest of the way home...will be seeing you in two or three weeks."

CROSSING POLECAT MOUNTAIN

My long journey had begun on November 20, 1942, with my induction into the Army at Ft. McPherson, Georgia. There I learned by bitter experience of the vendetta "Old Army" soldiers pursued vigorously against new enlisted recruits, especially those who had been drafted and those who admitted having high school diplomas and college degrees. As far as I was concerned, I had been drafted into Hell. The unstated official practice of the Army, if not the policy, seemed to be to take the civilian in, tear him down to the ground, then build him back up in the Army way. It was at "Ft. Mac" that I first experienced an Army physical examination including the embarrassing invasion by the manual digit, and the short arm inspection.

At the end of a grueling two weeks, I received assignment to the Army Air Force as a trainee for MOS 970, Link Trainer Operator, and was sent to Miami Beach for basic training. That was no vacation, Florida style. We were required to keep the apartments to which we were assigned free of dust and to do calisthenics in the thick sands until our feet were thoroughly blistered and raw, with no relief at sick call. I went on sick call only once in my entire Army experience. You didn't go to that place unless you were prepared to be insulted.

We were required to run up and down Collins Avenue at 4:00 a.m., shouting "hup, two, three, four" and singing "Off we go into the wild blue yonder…Hey nothing can stop the Army Air Corps," which the local citizenry would dearly have loved to do. We were assigned the most menial duties, scrubbing toilets, KP (washing pots and pans and peeling potatoes for the next meal). I did KP for eighteen hours on Christmas day,1942, while some crooner sang "I'm dreaming of a White Christmas" over the hotel audio system. This was in the basement of the McFadden-Deauville Hotel!

Episodes in the Life of a Bumpkin

By January 1, 1943, troop trains were bearing my group northward toward Chanute Field, Illinois, where a frigid winter was in progress. We were assigned two to a berth, including the upper. By lot, I drew an upper, outside assignment. An Army bent on punishing homosexuality put us in that predicament. About 2:00 a.m. the first night, I touched the outside wall which was an iceberg! I rebounded with such force as to send my berth-mate over the side, creating some belligerence in his heart. We both sat up the rest of the night. The second night, I told him the whole berth, in its entire paucity of space, was his, and welcome to it. Sleep wasn't worth the anxiety.

We arrived at Chanute Field with no warm clothing, but that deficiency was soon remedied. We were assigned to barracks, and my class in Link Trainer operation began. I almost flunked it before I made the mental transition from history-type language and expression to the highly technological terms of aeronautical flight.

It was at Chanute field that I learned the gutter language associated with dice-rolling, as the dice rolled against footlockers late into the night. "Eight, skate and donate, Nina from Pasadena, tear down the *bleep*-house Mama, I've lost my ass," etc. The sergeant would then awaken us at 4:00 A. M. shouting, "Drop your *bleeps* and grab your socks and be outside for formation in ten minutes." As my Army days rolled on, it became evident that gambling was rampant there, even on the troop ship going overseas. Later, a sergeant at my India base revealed that he had sent enough money home to buy a nice house, and he would continue to build his fortune for additional luxuries. Every payday evening, a crowd gathered at his basha either to watch or to gamble. As the evening wore on, we could hear yells about which parts of the anatomy had been lost. By midnight, the sergeant had all the money.

CROSSING POLECAT MOUNTAIN

The joke at Chanute Field was that your mama could be told to take down the flag, because no Link trainer operator had ever been sent overseas. If any soldier ever did that, he soon would have had to write mama to restore the flag. We had to do calisthenics daily, and I was punished by the Lieutenant in charge for not jumping correctly. He either didn't know, or chose to ignore, the fact that my right foot turns outward at about a twenty degree angle and wouldn't act correctly in jumping and marching. I didn't tell him. He was puzzled when I continued to jump erratically!

Some lighter moments punctuated those objectionable ones. A waitress at one of the base restaurants knocked an open bottle of syrup off the table into my lap. I had done nothing to insult her, so I guess it was an accident. She begged forgiveness and offered to have my uniform cleaned. Whether accidental or intentional, that was a sticky situation. I had only two uniforms, so I stayed away from restaurants until I got the sticky one back from the cleaners.

My major professor at Emory University, James Harvey Young, arranged for me to have lunch with Dr. and Mrs. J. G. Randall. Dr. Randall was a famous Lincoln scholar at the University of Illinois in Urbana, a few miles south of the base. I got the necessary permit to leave the base and began preparation to be on my best behavior. I met the two really gracious Randalls, and we sat down at a local restaurant to a delicious meal. I am too embarrassed to tell the rest of it. My fate must have been Douglas's revenge. Dr. Randall had one of his students show me around the campus, a scholar named David Herbert Donald who later wrote an updated version of the Lincoln story. In my career, I always operated in the shadows of the great.

I mentioned earlier that Rachel came to see me for one brief visit while I was at Chanute. I went to the nearest hotel to make a reservation for her visit. The clerk was a skinny little jerk. I was, too, of course. He looked me over and informed me that he ran a decent hotel and that if I brought a girl in there, I had better be prepared to show him a wedding certificate! I wrote Rachel to bring ours. He looked surprised when we presented it. Must have been a lot of sexual sinners around there, though I was told that most of them went east about fifty miles or north to a little town just south of Chicago. One man from Santa Barbara, California had a friend in Champaign whose wife, he bragged, was most accommodating. When I expressed shock that he would take advantage of a friend in that manner, he said "Look, Roy (my army name), if you can't *bleep* your friends, who can you *bleep*?

Our schooling over, our troop train rolled westward in early April. We stopped briefly in Albuquerque where a pigeon dropped his load on the shoulder of my freshly cleaned and pressed jacket. This led a scoffer to proclaim that I had been dubbed a colonel without applying. From there we went to Camp Luna for a few days where an impression was made for a dental device to substitute for the teeth that had been extracted at Chanute. The device was to follow me overseas.

We proceeded quickly through Oakland, California, where I drank my first beer and smoked my first cigarette, then to San Francisco where we boarded the 36,000-ton *Nieuw Amsterdam,* which had been converted to a troop carrier. It was full, over 5,000 of us, I think, with various MOSs and destinations. As we moved westward from the Golden Gate Bridge, a salute from the aft cannon shook the earth. My circulatory system malfunctioned, as did every other system I had. My fears were that the Japanese had gotten me before I had been given the opportunity to make Rachel and my parents proud by dying on some distant battlefield in the service of my fatherland. I was still a jerk.

We sailed southwest, and it was on this leg of the journey that we crossed the equator for the first time. There a ceremony was performed for us to appease Neptune or Poseidon, depending on one's preference for Roman or Greek Mythology.

The ceremony was revealing. The arrangement was that nurses' quarters were on the deck above the promenade deck. Enlisted personnel were quartered in the bowels of the ship. They might ascend to the promenade deck, but only male officers were pure enough to climb to the lofty heights of sacred feminine virtue, and, of course, only for the purpose of protecting the angels of mercy.

A male major conducted the party. He removed his jacket to prepare for the discharging of his duties. A comely nurse in blouse and shorts cavorted with the major. I don't know what her rank was. She didn't have her uniform on. As enlisted men looked heavenward, the major ran a garden hose under one leg of the nurse's shorts, and then down her blouse, with copious flow of water both ways. We supposed that was done to prove to Neptune that utter cleanliness prevailed amongst female passengers. Enlisted men were, of course, unmoved. The major was simply doing his duty as an officer and gentleman.

There were moments for reflection on this leg of the journey. For the first time I saw foxfire, alongside a ship. I saw flying fish and marveled at their beauty. I saw the intriguing wake trailing far behind a ship. And I wondered what could be the meaning of a war my generation had been taught was wrong.

There were less romantic moments. On May 14, 1943, I wrote what I then called a poem! A part of it was:

"I get up in the morning feeling fresh as the breeze.
Yeah, man, I'm ready to go.
I've had a night's sleep on the ship's high deck
Out of the slums on C Deck below.
At seven sharp I'm invited in
To beautiful mess No. 2.
But I'm stopped right off, must have done a grave sin,
Oh yes! *Bleep bleep it* get in columns of two.
Finally, I'm seated, packed in like sardines,
The orderly says that it must be done.
Seven men to the side, life jackets, canteens,
Oh, hell it's a lot of fun.
I look for some food to give me strength,
God knows I need strength in my legs.
But I look at the table across its full length
And see nothing but dry bread, raw bacon and eggs.

Soon we stopped overnight at Wellington, New Zealand, then by-passed Hobart, Tasmania, and stopped at Freemantle, Australia. The stay there was brief, too, and we began the most hazardous leg of our journey, a zig-zag trip northward through the Indian Ocean. When a log or something hit the hull where I was trying to sleep on C Deck, once again, I thought it was over for me. But at least Rachel and my parents could rejoice now that I had died in the line of duty in the service of my country as a result of enemy action.

Our next stop was Colombo, Ceylon (now Sri Lanka), where the India group left the *Nieuw Amsterdam* and went ashore for several days. The *Nieuw Amsterdam* continued to some other destination and I didn't hear of it again during the war years. I understand a sleek new version now sails on the Holland-America Lines.

When my group re-boarded, it was on three cattle boats, said to have been captured from Italy by the British. The cattle had been removed, but the pungent odor had not. As we steamed in more ways than one up the west coast of India, south of Bombay we hit a violent storm that lasted several days. The smell of cow manure and urine and the pitch and yaw sent many of my fellow travelers to the railing to feed the fish. I doubt that the fish ate it. Nothing sent me on that mission until, on the way to breakfast, I observed a barefoot cook drop a sausage on a sloppy floor, pick it up and put it back on the tray going to the dining area. Even that did not send me to the railing, but when I started to put a dried prune in my mouth and a white worm crawled out, I was on my way.

The terrible odor, unsanitary conditions throughout, and inedible food caused us to do something we never would have dreamed of earlier. We asserted our rights and issued a list of impossible demands. It should have been in our hearts to recognize that the management couldn't clean up the ship while the storm was raging. That ship could not have been cleaned anyway without tearing it down to the keel and starting over. As we exited the storm, we were called to topside and, looking up to the bridge, we heard the British commander yell,

"Last evening, someone broke into the store and stole the King's liquor."
"*Bleep Bleep* the King," came a shout from our midst.
"Who said that," demanded a U. S. second lieutenant standing by the commander."
"I did," a burly G. I. shouted, stepping forward to plain view. We applauded him.

"I say young man," the commander yelled, "You would not speak of President Roosevelt that way."

"*Bleep bleep* Roosevelt," came a quick retort. Again, we applauded.

We were soon told by the U. S. lieutenant that when we next docked, all three hundred of us would face courts martial. I don't think he really meant that, but he had to say something to appease a furious British officer. Nothing more was ever said about discipline of any kind. It seems, too, that some of our most furious had been to "prayer" with the lieutenant about his post-war plans.

We docked at Bombay, and, after a delicious meal in a famous hotel, including delectable chocolate goodies, we returned to ship. It was in Bombay that I first encountered the pitiful beggars, the "no mama, no papa, baksheesh, sahib" syndrome, and those trying to sell us an encounter with their "sisters" or "mamas" for a small amount of rupees.

We sailed north to Karachi, and that proved to be my last experience in ocean surface travel. I had traveled on water 16,000 miles and didn't know how to swim! My parents had not even allowed me to go to the swimming holes in the creek. We stayed in a staging area outside Karachi for about two weeks. On our truck ride to the staging area, we observed a phenomenon of more than passing interest, a naked woman parading on the sidewalk. We were told she was protesting something. Her appearance lent credence to the suggestion that she might be protesting her own physique. Betel nut juice on her teeth added the thought that she might have been slapped hard in the mouth by a disgruntled husband or suitor. We all agreed that as far as we were concerned, she raised no prurient interest.

At the staging area, we in the lower ranks of enlisted men were again subjected to humiliation and scorn. For instance, one could not be assigned KP or guard duty by persons of higher rank, mostly "Old Army" uneducated sergeants and officers, without a smirking statement, such as,

"Cox, I'm really embarrassed to assign a college graduate to such lowly duty, but...." I would have accepted the assignment more willingly if given without the sarcasm. Finally, a day or so before our departure for the bowels of India, I was assigned to a desk job for a day so that the non-commissioned officers could go into town. As the final blow at Karachi, violent dysentery became epidemic, probably Gandhi's revenge. At 2:00 A. M. I found it expedient to exit my basha and proceed in great haste to the latrine at the edge of the area.

"Halt" shouted the guard.

"Halt, hell, I yelled back over my shoulder. "I haven't got time to halt."
"Halt, or I'll shoot," came the insensitive command.
"*Bleep bleep it,*" I yelled. "If you've got to shoot, go ahead. If I don't get to the latrine in a hurry, I'm dead anyway."

I don't think he shot. If he had, I wouldn't have felt it or heard it.

We were herded into C-46s that somehow rattled up into the air and headed east, destination unknown. They were equipped with parachutes, and we strapped them on. We landed at Agra for refueling, but were not permitted to visit the Taj Mahal, not enough time. From there, we went to Chabua, headquarters for "Hump" operations. That was sometime in early June, 1943, I think. My fellow Link Trainer Operators and I were soon transferred to Jorhat, then a short time later some of us were sent on down the Brahmaputra River to Tezpur. There I began the first of three monsoon seasons I was to be there. Eventually, the base at Tezpur became the 1327 Army Air Force Base Unit (AAFBU).

Soon after we arrived at Tezpur, I wrote the following lines as a part of my poem "Woes of a Sad Sack."

>He arrived in India, oh unhappy day
>How long, he said, do I have to stay?
>And the old GIs who had been there for years
>Gave him the news that brought him to tears.
>He'd be right there till his eyes were glazed
>And he walked unconsciously, bewildered and dazed.
>Then he found that his job just wasn't there.
>Oh, dejected soul, he lives in despair.

We were told immediately that the shipment of Link Trainers, originally destined for the Assam Valley, India, which we were in, had found a final resting place at the bottom of the Indian Ocean and that it would be at least eight months before another shipment could arrive. Perhaps until this day "The dark unfathomed caves of ocean bear" our much-needed equipment. (Apologies to Gray). It seemed to me to be fortunate that our machines were there, and not us.

A merciful commanding officer looked around for something Link Trainer Operators could do other than policing the area, guard duty, or KP. I was assigned to a major in G-2, Intelligence. I typed his memos, that were either in some disarmingly simple code or said nothing. At least it gave me something to do while we waited for our machines. I was embarrassed, chagrined, and ground into dust one afternoon when the major asked me to work late and I protested that I would be late for chow. That put him in the mood to put me in my place. "Well, Corporal Cox, I just wanted you to type my recommendation for your promotion to sergeant." He let me go to chow, which wasn't worth the loss of a promotion that would make Rachel and my parents so proud! He also allowed me to squirm all night, then the next morning, with a wry grin, handed me the recommendation to type. The other four operators who arrived at Tezpur with me received similar assignments. Ennui set in, driving me to write my poem, "India."

> India Land—land of mystery
> Land with years of romantic history
> Land where the hot sun bakes your brains
> Land where it rains, and rains, and rains
> Land where the dust gets in your eyes
> While you stand in mud up to your thighs
> Land where the heat rash burns and galls
> And you scratch the hair right   *bleep*
> Land where you try to get some sleep
> While millions of insects around you creep
> Land of beautiful pleasant dreams
> While sweat pours off you in ceaseless streams
> Land where cowbells long have rung
> And you walk down the streets through piles of dung
> Land of lovely cluttered cities
> Where the women wear sackcloth 'round their *bleeps*
> Land where the liqueurs are quite all right
> Drink, you can't do worse than lose your sight
> Land where it's hard as hell to eat
> This constant diet of buffalo meat
> Wonderful, my friends, wherever you roam
> You'll never find a place so much like home.

Episodes in the Life of a Bumpkin

Monsoons were a new experience for me. Georgia's "two-week wet spells" were in comparison a single drop. I seldom visited the Tezpur laundry. I just wore my clothes, stink and all. After all, I wasn't going to date a native girl or hug a man. When I did break loose and send clothes to the laundry, they came back stinking and laced with mildew. It was too rainy to hang our uniforms out to sun, so the mildew accumulated. But what did it matter? Appearances were that we would never get back home. Pessimism pervaded the spirit.

Eventually, I think about May, 1944, we got our Link Trainer machines and set up shop in a largely open, basha-like structure with a thatched roof, bamboo siding, and all that. The dampness was devastating on the bellows that powered the movements in the cockpit. We were forced to do rear echelon maintenance without any training for it. Sergeant Bob Pritchard of Pennsylvania was our leader and kept our schedules and other duties straight.

Why did we need Link Trainers over there anyway? The reason was that pilots had been sent over there with little or no instrument training. And when four-engine craft arrived, transition training from two to four engine planes had to be done on the spot. This involved even more "blind flying" training if the pilots had not had it stateside.

In addition, General W. H. Tunner was soon to arrive and order flying in all weather and at nights. Our job was to assist in training untrained, or under-trained, pilots for instrument flight. This was not always a welcome service as pilots saw it, but our flight captain did much to remedy any friction. He saw that unless we flew with the pilots and saw their problems aloft, there would be a gap in understanding. So, although the practice might be questioned somewhere up the line of command, he scheduled Link Trainer

Operators to make flights across the Hump as observers. Since we were unofficial passengers, we were not on flight pay, and, as far as I know, were not listed on the manifest. I often wondered if we were in one of the sad crashes how long it would be before Rachel and my parents were made proud, if at all. Somebody on the base knew and would have told eventually. We accepted these assignments willingly, because it did ease the atmosphere among pilots, who were bearing the brunt of Hump flights, and operators. But, after being on a flight to Chengdu, China, I would not advise anyone to eat scrambled eggs there. I did, just once!

Our duty was to haul gasoline over the Hump to our forces on the other side. At first, this was done almost exclusively in C-46s and C-47s carrying 55-gallon drums. Later, C-109 tankers did part of the work. There was steady upgrading of the types of craft needed after General Tunner arrived.

He arrived in early August 1944 to assume command of Hump operations. He assessed the problems of excessive casualties, low troop morale, and low tonnage deliverance and moved quickly to lower these deficiencies, all the while balancing pressures from Washington and those from Generals Chenault, Wedemeyer and other high ranking "brass" in the theater. He was billed as "the man who moved anything, anywhere, any time," and he just about did over there. He found personnel pretty well demoralized. He wrote in discussing supplies, "In many respects, the entire command was just plain forgotten."

He gave this example with respect to food. The General heard on a regular news broadcast while flying over the area on Thanksgiving Day, 1944 that the armed forces were providing turkey for all American troops overseas. "I licked my lips," he said, but when he landed at one of the bases he commanded and went to officers' mess, he found wienies and sauerkraut! He concluded: "This was the Hump. We were at the end of the line." That explains pretty well why those of us who had been there a while were demoralized.

General Tunner was one of those rare administrators who knew Army regs well, but also knew when to take them under advisement and do what he had to do to get his job done. From my enlisted man viewpoint, he made a few errors in judgment. For example, he wrote, "I saw to it that a fair and dependable system of rotation for everyone was put into effect." If he did, it never reached the 1327 AAFBU in Tezpur. The system said that one who accumulated a certain number of months and points would be rotated. The catch was that a replacement with a similar MOS had to be on base first. No such person ever came to replace a Link Trainer Operator on our base. If Truman had not ended the war with Japan, I would be buried somewhere between Tezpur and Tokyo or, at best, paddling a dinghy up and down the Brahmaputra River. In fairness, I must admit that General Tunner also said, "It was not an easy system to work out, I discovered later." He never did get it perfected.

Yet another flaw in his judgment was his insistence on stateside military courtesy. This significant quotation reveals my point:

> "I went ahead with my full-scale program. The men stood inspection and marched in parades and shaved their faces and cut their hair and spruced up both their personal appearance and their living quarters. Military courtesy was no longer just a phrase. I had been sent to this command to direct American Soldiers, and while I was their commander, by God, they were going to live like Americans and be proud they were Americans."

CROSSING POLECAT MOUNTAIN

Live like Americans over there?

What an "Old Army" General could not realize was that respect and pride have little or nothing to do with lining up in rows and acting like puppets. Our base officers had not required such folderol, and we respected them, worked hard for them, and, of course, we were proud to be Americans before the General arrived. We just wanted to get our jobs done and get back home.

The General's discipline had some interesting effects at Tezpur. Few of us had been trained well in the use of weapons. Some of us had received weapons instruction in basic training and knew how to aim, fire, and go through inspection procedures. Some had not. In one of the heralded inspections, the inspecting lieutenant stopped before each and gave whatever the command was, to do whatever was supposed to be done, with the weapon in hand. Some had .45 pistols, some had M1 rifles, some had Carbines. When he gave the command to a short little communications soldier, who had a .45, a mighty blast shattered the air. It seemed forever before the lieutenant could speak. His face was as if bleached by the thundering India sun under which we stood. When his voice returned, his only command was, "at ease, fallout." We almost did fall, laughing.

Another incident involved a major fresh from our homeland, and me. He demanded respect. He and I approached a bamboo clump from opposite directions, and I prepared to give my most respectful salute. As I reached the proper distance, I did. His reply was about halfway up when a cobra that appeared long enough to reach from Tezpur to Karachi slithered out between us. His arm dropped, he effected a sharp about face and with a "goddam, sergeant" fled unceremoniously. I retreated a respectable distance and watched the reptile until it posed no danger to me. I never knew where the major went or whether the reptile exulted in its power over the military!

There were other incidents. A lieutenant colonel, recently from Washington, ordered us around like a cattle round-up. He appeared one morning with his head severely lacerated. Official word was that he was unfamiliar with his new surroundings and had fallen into a deep ditch trying to find his new quarters. Whatever happened, he was not seen again in our area.

We had an African-American unit out at the edge of the base, under the command of a white captain. The captain was said by black soldiers to be a terror, somewhat less than holy. Once, the captain ordered me to drive him in his jeep to the unit. That was not a part of my assigned job, but it was an order. As we entered the basha area, a shout rang out, "Sergeant, don't bring that *bleep bleeped* son of a bitch in here." I looked pleadingly at the captain. No relief. He ordered me to go on in. I figured I was about to die in the line of duty, but neither side shot at me. "Touched by an angel," I suppose, in the middle of Hell. A few days later, word came that the captain had been sliced about the face with a razor. About six weeks later, I saw him in the PX, and scars proved he had truly been sliced. He talked freely about it and was soon rotated out. Such incidents were not condoned. In my opinion, they were the result of utter frustration, of a feeling that we had really been forgotten and didn't matter in the war effort. In addition to being forgotten, now we had chicken *bleep*. This frustration, I think, led to some incidents such as those described immediately above, which were shameful and should never have happened.

Most of our officers were great men. They treated enlisted personnel as if they believed we were all in India to help win the war for America. We were proud of them and I think they of us. In my approximately two years in Tezpur, enough happened to fill a large library if it had been recorded. Some examples follow:

My dental prosthesis caught up with me in Tezpur, or at least I thought so. I reported to the dentist as ordered. As he removed the device from the package, we discovered that I had been sent a full set of dentures. What the poor fellow somewhere gumming it did with my partial was never brought to my attention, and I never saw my partial! That was SNAFU! (Translation later).

In Ken W. Thomas's article "Southern Route to India," he mentions that Jinx Falkenburg and Pat O'Brien were fellow passengers on a part of his trip in 1944. They stopped at Tezpur either on their way to Burma or on their return. I was there when they arrived and sat with hundreds of others, in the big outdoor arena, to hear their performance. I was also there after O'Brien and Falkenburg when Paulette Goddard and Keenan Wynn dropped by to raise our morale. Of course, enlisted folks had to sit so far back that we could barely see them, but the loudspeaker worked. Paulette was squired around the base by our commanding officer, and this was said to be the arrangement at all of Paulette's stops. Shortly after her return to the United States, some magazine that was distributed to the CBI, *Time*, I think, reported that she had undergone a stomach operation.

Airplane accidents, sadly, were routine. We were sitting in the Monsoon Bowl one night, watching a film warning us about "Miss Anopheles" and malaria, when a C-46 labored down the runway and the dreaded thump, thump, boom occurred. Everybody ran to the rice paddy, but it was too late to help. All were dead except the radio operator, who was sitting on a paddy divider rubbing his singed head. He died in the base hospital a few hours later. The stabilizer chocks had not been removed. "Miss Anopheles" was mild compared to a burning plane with our buddies in it. On another occasion while sitting in the same Bowl, we saw a massive flash of white to the west. This time the plane had gained altitude, but a spark from somewhere set the drums of gasoline afire, blowing the craft to bits and killing another fine crew.

Another incident that should not have happened, but did anyway, involved a pilot who, on the spur of the moment, decided to have some fun and buzz officers' quarters. As he brought his four-engine craft in over the enlisted area, lowering more and more toward the officers' area, he hooked into a clump of bamboo and ripped an engine out of its moorings. He landed safely with the other three engines, and no crew member was hurt. We heard that he was fined five hundred dollars for his frivolity. A sergeant, gambling with his Captain, had an accident with his .45, shot his Captain in the stomach, and was also fined five hundred dollars.

My recollection is that a good bit of local booze was consumed. There was an especially potent libation. I think it had the word "Applejack" in its name. My memory is that this libation was to the imbiber's insides as the A-Bomb was to Hiroshima and Nagasaki. I saw more than one of my fellow Tezpurians fall out after drinking the stuff. I didn't drink it, not because I was good and pure, but because I still had a faint glimmer of hope that someday I would return to my homeland.

After stateside beer began making its way to the Assam Valley, I drank my ration, for several months hot! Budweiser is pretty tasty that way! Finally, a crew came through and set up an ice maker. A sort of NCO club was established, and we deposited our beer there to be cooled and checked out later. My beer led to an interesting encounter.

I found a wallet in the road with no identification in it. What was in it was a considerable number of Indian rupees. I could have easily kept the money and thrown the wallet back in the road where I found it, but somehow my old North Georgia sense of fairness took over. One just didn't keep something one knew wasn't his. I went immediately to headquarters and turned it over to the executive officer. He took the wallet and my base address. What he might want with my exact address caused me some concern, but surely he wouldn't accuse me of grand theft or something, so I forgot it. Some days later, there was a knock at the door of our humble basha.

One of my basha mates answered the knock. I was sitting at a small table writing Rachel when a booming voice demanded, "Is Sergeant Cox in here?" Ten hut was sounded when the voice was identified as that of an officer. What have I done now, thought I. Although he was only a second lieutenant, he could get me busted with just a word or two at headquarters. My wife and parents would never understand. I jumped to attention, turning my little makeshift table over. I identified myself with all the dignity I could muster. Yes, Sir, Cox, Roy L. Jr., Sir, 20586015. (number false). The welcome command, "At ease, Sergeant," calmed me reasonably well. Explaining that he would be ever grateful for the return of his wallet, he began peeling off rupee notes as my reward. My response was that I wished no reward and in good conscience could not accept one.

He returned the money to his wallet, but he tempted me further. "Sergeant," he said, "I see you have written a letter there that must go through censors. Hand me the envelope, and in the future bring all of your letters sealed to my basha and I will approve them unopened." He had undermined my pride. He had made me an offer I could not refuse. He crushed my resistance once again. "Sergeant, I see you have a case of beer there. I don't know why in hell I can't get beer. I will be so grateful if you will bring your beer and I will swap you my ration of Bourbon for it." I would have preferred Scotch, but he had my principles hawg tied. I immediately accepted his offer of Bourbon. After dark, as he had suggested, I lugged my entire case of Budweiser over across the ditch to his basha and received ample Bourbon in return. Then he poured some of his Basha mate's ration, and we had a long conversation about families and backgrounds and plans for the future. I never took advantage of his friendship. I respected the distance that must be maintained between officers and enlisted men. I felt tremendous pride in our mutual trust and respect. Eventually, he flew his allotted missions across the hump, and rotated. After that, I lost sight of him, unfortunately, even his name, but my pleasant memories of him remain steadfast. For some reason, he trusted me.

Booze along the Brahmaputra sometimes produced ludicrous effects. We were awakened one night by a violent earthquake which bound us so tightly to our charpoys that we couldn't get out—except that the basha drunk did. As we realized the dangers that faced us, he was standing in the doorway shouting, "Get up and stand in the doorway, boys. You'll be safer there!" There was only one door in the basha, and he was in it! He prayed, "Lord, I know I'm drunk, but you know I'm a long way from home and haven't seen my wife and kids for more than a year. Have mercy, Oh Lord!" Mercy was applied. The shaking ceased before the basha fell in. On another occasion, that of a Jap air raid, his constant state of inebriation allowed him to wobble into the slit trench nearest us before the rest of us could get there.

CROSSING POLECAT MOUNTAIN

That earthquake was one of the two I experienced while at Tezpur. The other, in daytime, shook me to the ground where I squirmed to get up, but failed. Fortunately, the earth did not open up where I lay. It did crack elsewhere on our base, but as far as I know no soldier fell in. It opened up in a big way about two hundred miles to the northeast, I heard later.

As mentioned earlier, we had had no training for combat. The nature of the weapon we had varied for person to person. I had a carbine. Back in time somewhere, we had been issued two rounds of ammunition, but most of us had lost those. They were too hard to keep up with. I managed to keep my two bullets for the purpose of guarding myself against tiger attacks when forced to visit the latrine. In a tight spot, either the tiger or I would have been shot. Our situation became more binding when the Japanese army crossed the border from Burma into India in 1944. We were all taken to the edge of a rice paddy and assigned a post to defend if Tezpur were to be attacked. We were issued three more rounds of ammunition. No tiger having had the temerity to attack me, I had become lax and lost my first two, so I had only the three. Even if I, and everyone else, made all three of those good, we were dead ducks anyway, and everybody knew it. As General Tunner wrote, we were at the end of the line with no place to hide. Fortunately for us, the British stopped the Japanese before they reached us.

Another result of the combat threat was fear of sabotage, and this led to guard duty way out in a lonely revetment where our planes were parked. We were each assigned to a plane and given the commands to issue before any shooting. We were to protect our plane at all cost to us personally. The penalty for dereliction of duty was said to be Fort Leavenworth for life. One corporal of the guard decided to try me. He almost went too far. I still shudder every time I think of it. He was in one of our Army jeeps, but that was not absolute proof of his legitimacy. We had been told that Japanese soldiers could steal jeeps, so watch out. I shouted out all of the prescribed commands, yet the corporal wouldn't stop. He just kept coming straight at me and my plane. As my finger embraced the trigger of my carbine and I took aim, he identified himself and laughed at me. But for a steadiness of nerve that I never claimed to have, he would have been dead, and I would have rotted in Leavenworth or, perhaps, have been executed. The latter would have been preferable.

The Kansas facility was brought frequently to our attention, especially for the crime of homosexuality. The base bulletin board carried notices of courts martial, quite a number of which announced 20 years in Leavenworth for some soldier who had carnal relations per **anum,** usually with a male citizen of India. Once a clerk typed that the Leavenworth bound culprit had carnal relations per **annum.** The soldier was known in our area of the base, and we remarked that the poor joker had only been there seven or eight months. We should not have joked about it, but it was hard to find anything at all to joke about over there.

"End of the line" food was almost edible. We improvised where possible. We had a constant diet of atabrine and other stuff. The meal I coveted most was a large plate of fried okra. I wrote home for some okra seed, got them, and planted them behind my basha. My crop grew unusually well, and in due time blossomed and produced the delectable pods. Now to get it cooked while it was still young and tender. I took a few cans of my beer ration for that month to the mess hall boys and bartered for some meal and some cooking oil. They had never heard of okra and weren't interested in acquainting themselves with it. Certainly, they wouldn't cook that "crap" for me. They finally relented and gave me what I needed, including a small frying pan. I returned to the basha to prepare my delicacy. I had bought a small stove in Tezpur.

The loud guffaws of derision could have been heard all the way to Calcutta, or up in Darjeeling if anyone had bothered to look up and listen. "What is that stuff?" they asked. "Cox, you have lost your damned mind." I chose not to debate their evaluation of my mental state. I pressed steadily ahead, carefully cutting my tender pods, then rolling the product in meal, thence to the heated oil in the frying pan. The aroma was absolutely heavenly. As I browned my okra just right, my detractors gathered close, one by one. They tasted. "Best stuff I've had since leaving the States," they murmured. I got so little of that first cooking that I was more discreet and secretive as my stalks continued to bear. I simply could not feed all the converted Yankees!

There were dietary differences between Muslims and Hindus. Their differences covered many facets of life. Our basha cleaner, a Muslim, rushed out of the basha one day and fiercely attacked a Hindu passing by. When I asked what that was all about, he explained to me that his victim was a Hindu and thus a bad man. I replied that religion can be a very dangerous thing. He appeared not to comprehend my meaning.

It was hard to evaluate native citizens. Their existence and ours were pretty much separate. From a distance, they seemed to me to have close to the same values as ours. Maybe they were sometimes ahead of us in concepts of honor and integrity. They objected strongly when their wives and daughters, working around the base, were called "Bebe" by insensitive soldiers. The word carried an unfavorable connotation. They objected to any suggestion, by word or deed, that we considered them inferior human beings. We were their guests, only slightly mistrusted because we were helping the British, whom they tolerated but did not love. Their wages were exceedingly low on the British pay scales. For instance, we paid Indian workers on the base considerably more than they could make picking tea leaves, which caused some friction between soldier and planter.

There were tea planters who were most kind to us, inviting a few soldiers at a time to their elaborate compounds for a few days of rest and relaxation. I was included in such an invitation to the plantation supervised by Mr. and Mrs. Guy O'Connell-Hefke. They were splendid folks. They showed us the entire operation they supervised, including picking the tea and processing it. The leaves were dried. Then there was elaborate tasting of the brew the leaves generated. In that process, we learned that only the tender leaves were picked, irrespective of which vendor put its label on it.

While there, we ate tree-ripened bananas and sipped hot tea with our hosts several times a day. We swapped purloined C-rations for an extra bounty of fried chicken. At night, the servant boy was ordered to draw our baths, a fresh one for each visitor. Clean water, warmed to just the right temperature, provided a luxury I had never heard of. In fact, this was my first tub bath, unless you count the wash tub in which I, with great contortions, took my baths at home on Saturday nights. We had showers in college, but never tubs! The whole experience was a wonderful one. We discussed the war effort, lack of massive United States equipment in the CBI, Dunkirk, and the difference, if any, between aluminum and aluminium. Up there and back, we saw the multitude of wild animals that inhabited the countryside. Elephants, tigers, and other wild beasts roamed freely in the jungles and open areas. They seemed happy and didn't bother us.

Back at the base, we again encountered reality. We slept night after night under our mosquito nets, sweating gallons while listening to the concerts of the beasts and birds out in the nearby jungle, set to the cadence of native drums. No mechanical recorder could ever have captured those sounds, sounds recorded only in the souls of the hearers.

Snakes were more than plentiful. We didn't worry as much about the cobra as we did about the krait, a very small snake that had the mischievous habit of crawling into one's shoes during the night and gnawing the toe of the unwary soldier who might be groggy enough in the morning to put his shoe on without shaking it first. We were told in orientation sessions that a krait bite was fatal in about eight seconds. In my basha, we all beat our shoes on the ground and shook them vigorously. Of course, the python was around, too, but I never saw one of those. Tales were told of one eighteen feet long and its encounter with a local citizen. As it backed out of its den, the citizen obliged society by cutting it into short pieces with his trusty gurkha knife, so that when it finally had exposed its whole self, it had only a head, no end! Mongooses could usually kill snakes, but I saw only one such encounter, and it was staged.

Monkeys were the menace of our bashas. They would get between the thatched roof and the white cloth ceiling and take care of certain urges. We had to protect the top of our mosquito nets with whatever material we could find to keep unwanted liquids from falling through on us. Since we would have violated Indian customs to kill the monkeys, we had to put up with the monkeying around. Finally, mid-August 1945 and VJ day came. I, as many others did, went to the "Club" that night and checked out my beer, 12 cans as I recall, and, again, as I recall, I drank it. Some hours later, I was fundamentally sick. Why would I do such a stupid thing? There is no logical answer.

As dawn opened, we got orders to pack our bags and be ready to leave. About 9:00 a.m., one of General Tunner's infamous parades was ordered for 11:00 a.m. The sun had come up like thunder and our throbbing heads responded in kind. We couldn't hear and we couldn't see. The Noel Coward song that says something like "Mad dogs and Englishmen go out in the mid-day sun" certainly fit us that day. We were the mad dogs, slobbering and stumbling from a night of debauchery. That was TARFU. But we made it through, thank Bacchus, I suppose. The Christian God would not have known us.

That afternoon or the next morning, we reported in groups, as ordered, to learn our departure schedule. To our surprise and utter shock, some of us were being assigned to China. It turned out that most of them so assigned had been in the CBI only a short time. But I was in that group. My guts froze. Twenty-seven months in purgatory, and I hadn't worked myself upward. Instead, I was now assigned to Hell on the lowest ring. We had all talked about what was happening in the internal politics of China and the bloodshed that would be involved. It was hard to tell which side any one Chinese citizen was on, loyalist or communist. What would a Link Trainer Operator do over there? I could guess. Would he be given a Carbine and three rounds of ammunition and assigned to a rice paddy to defend? I felt that I was on the River Styx near the point of no return.

I was ordered to report to supply and pick up chemical warfare uniforms, then pack my belongings and be ready to leave the following morning. I complied, but I was in a state of absolute depression. I must have been albino white. One soldier I thought was my friend laughed and said, "What's the matter, Cox, are you scared?" The truth was that I was much more angry than scared. I was so angry with my country that I would have defected, but there was no place to defect to! The severe blow had subordinated my judgment. That was FUBAR, the end. Not only was there no light at the end of the tunnel, but the tunnel had caved in on me and crushed every spark of hope I had nurtured through three monsoons. The sun no longer shone above the clouds. I would never see my family again.

When morning opened, I was summoned to headquarters. Why? What other insult could await me? That question rang through my mind at every step as I walked the quarter mile or so to headquarters. I reported to the officer whose name was on the slip of paper delivered to me. I managed a snappy salute and the required protocol: "Staff Sergeant Cox, Roy L. Jr, Sir, reporting as ordered, Sir."

"Sergeant, I've been looking over this China list, and a mistake was made by the clerk. You don't belong on this list. Prepare to leave for the States on the first available plane." I managed a salute, did an about face, and began the walk back to my basha. My emotions were then and still are indescribable. Back at the basha, I threw the chemical warfare clothing in a corner. It may still be there. My other belongings were made to conform to a list of items we could take back to the States. Weight limitations were severe—only a small duffel bag with bare essentials inside. I didn't care. I would have gone back home stark naked if that were required. But that would have been a sin.

Shortly, I was on a C-46 heading west. Five days later I was in Casablanca. I'm not sure where we stopped in India on the way, but Karachi was the point of our departure from India. (It would later become part of Pakistan, but that nation had not yet been imagined.) I had made many good friends in India, chief of which was a basha mate, Sergeant Jacob G. Stansbury of New Iberia, Louisiana. He was a great gentleman, loved his family and his God, and was a mighty inspiration to me.

We flew from Karachi, up the Persian Gulf to Abadan, and after a brief hot, hot stop there, we flew across the Arabian desert to Cairo. We followed the southern rim of the Mediterranean Sea, making brief stops at Tripoli and Oran. At Oran, we blew a tire on takeoff and nearly had a date with the sea. The tire repaired, we moved on to Casablanca. I think we were there about two weeks. Finally, we got a plane and flew south to Dakar.

In Dakar, we were able to pick up a C-54, a luxury liner compared to the C-46s we had been in all the way from Tezpur. We headed southwest. About fifteen minutes out of Dakar, just after we had been cleared to loosen our seatbelts, we hit an unexpected storm. Later, the co-pilot told us we had taken a free fall for 700 feet. With no seatbelts to restrain us, and improper securing of baggage above our heads, the plane's interior looked as if we had been in an all-night brawl. Some poor guy in the tail section had just lain down with a duffel bag as a pillow and had busted his nose on the top of the plane. Others were bruised in various places. I went straight to the top, almost stuck my head out for air, and came back down astraddle my seat arm. I cannot describe my agony. It seemed doubtful Rachel and I would ever have children.

Never again did I ride in a plane with my seatbelt unbuckled, even in cavu (ceiling and visibility unlimited) conditions. I could not stand another event like that one off the coast from Dakar.

CROSSING POLECAT MOUNTAIN

Here all three Acronyms expressing our disgust throughout the war came into play. SNAFU: "Situation normal, all fouled up. TARFU: Things are really fouled up. FUBAR: Fouled up beyond all recognition." "Fouled" is not exactly the word we used, but it will have to do here.

We straightened up, and ten long hours later, we landed in Natal, Brazil. We rested a while in some building that had bunks. Back on a C-46, we headed up the coast to Georgetown, San Juan, and at long last 36th Street Airport in Miami. I fell on my knees, thanked Almighty God, and kissed the oily tarmac. That was mid-September 1945.

And so, I had come full circle, from Lickskillet across to the fresh breezes of the other side of Polecat Mountain, through the enlightening atmosphere of Reinhardt and Emory, and through the good and the bad of serving my Country. I joined the hundreds of thousands of civilian soldiers who went when we were called, served the best we could, were discharged for the convenience of the Government, and proceeded to put our lives back together. Many were not so fortunate.

As the mighty winds of WWII began to subside in 1945, (I refer not to Franklin Roosevelt and Winston Churchill), we were asked to designate an Air Force base from which we would like to be discharged. Possible choices were supplied, and I checked Greensboro, North Carolina, or something Green up there. Whatever the base was, I never saw it. I was routed first to Cincinnati, from which I was dispatched to Greenwood, Mississippi, thence to Maxwell Air Force Base near Montgomery, Alabama. There we were finally reunited with our records, without which we would still be in the Army. After two days of intense pressure to enlist in the Army Reserve, my group decided to sever our ties with the Army altogether, and then we got those coveted discharge papers. Oh! I almost forgot. I was called to the paymaster's office to be told that my separation pay was somehow one hundred dollars short, and that if I would stick around two or three weeks, the money would be there to pay me that arrears amount---it surely would take no more than a month! I smiled my best smile and said thanks but no thanks. As I recall, I got my check in the mail about two months later.

From Montgomery, I caught a ride to Atlanta with another soldier who had somehow acquired an automobile. He dropped me off at the Greyhound bus station in Atlanta and was homeward bound when he discovered my stupid mistake. I had left my discharge papers in his car. In the meantime, back at the station, I was walking the floor, stunned and frantic. I didn't remember the man's name who had befriended me with the ride. So, there was no way I could get in touch with him. Wonderful luck befell me. About ten minutes before I was to board the bus to Chatsworth, Georgia, where my mountain Sweet Shrub was, that good and noble man walked into the station waving my papers. Had I the power, I would have canonized him on the spot.

The bus rolled along slowly but surely until we reached the little road that led through the woods to Mama Gregory's house. I awakened her and Rachel in the middle of the night, but they didn't seem to mind.

Evidences began to appear that returning soldiers were appreciated. A few days after I was reunited with Rachel, we rode over in her 1937 Ford to a Dalton restaurant. I was still wearing my uniform with the five hash marks on my sleeve indicating more than two years in foreign service. We ate a steak, and I went to the cashier to pay. She said, "Sir, your bill has been paid." Either the manager or some other appreciative citizen had paid for our meals.

Another incident that demonstrated appreciation happened when I went to see Dad and Mother. Rachel had a few more days of teaching to do before Christmas Holidays and could not accompany me. I rode the bus from Chatsworth to Marietta and don't remember how I got from Marietta to Woodstock. Anyway, I was there and needed a ride over the six miles to my childhood home, from which I had left for parts unknown three years earlier. I knew Mr. Sam Dawson who worked in a general store there, J. H. Johnston's I think, and inquired of him as to whether he knew of someone I could hire to take me the remaining distance. He said, "Son, there's no one around here you can hire—because I am going to take you." He did, and said to Dad, "Roy, look what I brought you." Dad leapt off the porch where he was sitting, literally ran to the edge of the yard, and for the first and last time in his life—hugged me! He had expected me to come home in a casket, if at all.

Photo Album
(Captioned from memory by Dargan Ware)

The seated women are R. Linton Cox's mother, Leila Foster Cox, on the viewer's left, and his wife, Rachel Gregory Cox, on the right. The standing woman is his daughter Evelyn Gregory Cox.

CROSSING POLECAT MOUNTAIN

Mr. Cox received the Service Above Self award from Rotary International, an organization of which he was an active member for many years and District Governor in the mid-1980's.

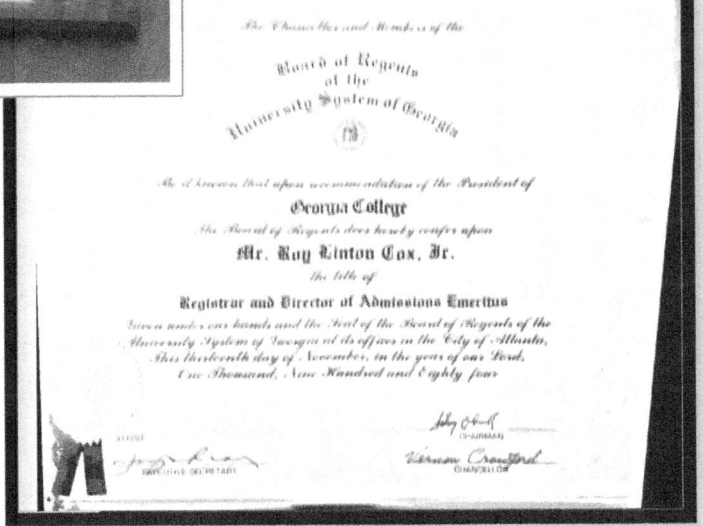

This award was presented to Mr. Cox by the University System of Georgia upon his retirement as Registrar and Director of Admissions at Georgia College, which was known as Women's College of Georgia when he began working there, and is now known as Georgia College and State University.

Episodes in the Life of a Bumpkin

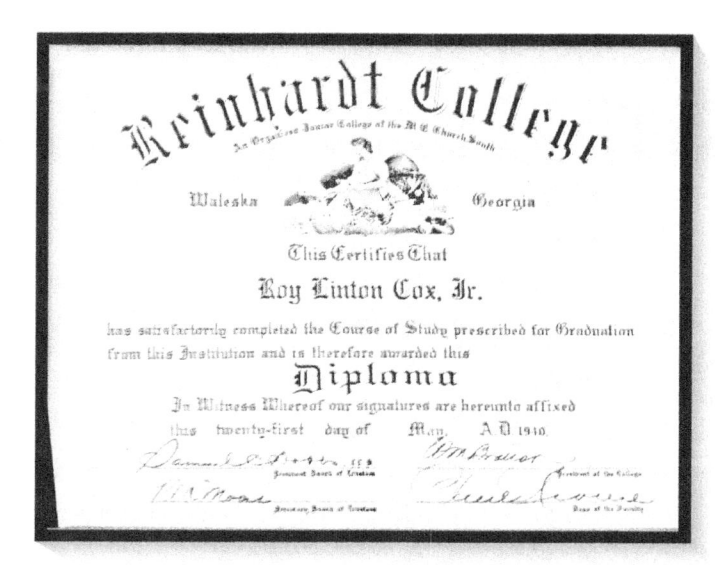

This is Mr. Cox's diploma from Reinhardt College in Waleska, Georgia, the place he initially "crossed Polecat Mountain" to reach.

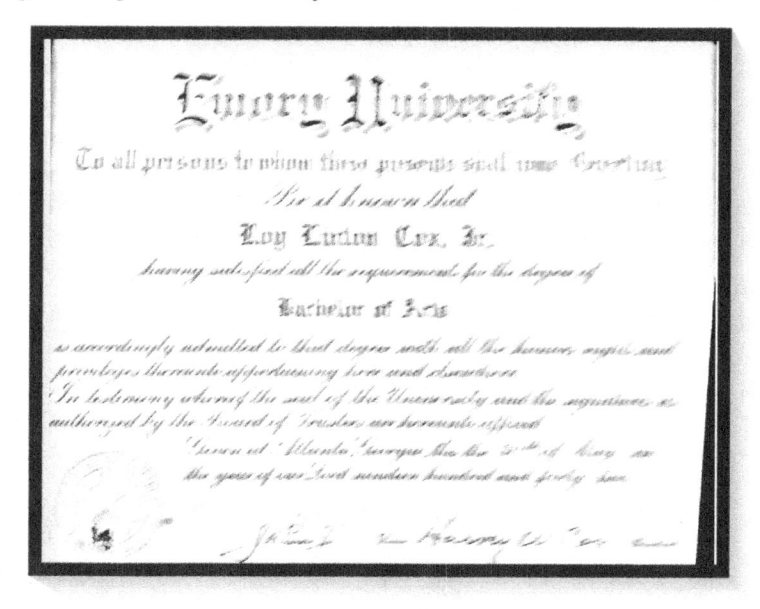

Pop's diploma from Emory University in Atlanta.

I believe this picture of Pop was taken about the time he served in India during World War II.

Linton and Rachel Cox around the time of their marriage, with him in his uniform from World War II.

Episodes in the Life of a Bumpkin

I believe this picture of Granny was taken near the time of her marriage to Pop.

This picture of a smiling Linton and Rachel Cox exemplifies the way I remember Pop and Granny in the late 80's or early 90's.

Rachel Gregory Cox, Pop's "Sweet Mountain Shrub"

Episodes in the Life of a Bumpkin

Linton and Rachel Cox and their children (from left to right for the viewer) Evelyn, Vivian, and Linton, taken in the early 70's. Their oldest daughter Lillian is not pictured.

VALDOSTA

AS I CAST MY LINE OUT FOR A JOB, one fell into my lap! Emory University was re-opening a junior college division in Valdosta, Georgia. The division had been closed during the war years. In staffing the resurrected division, the History Department from which I had just graduated was asked to turn up a social studies candidate. The Department turned me up, either because I was the prime choice of the Department, or because all the other graduates had been placed. In either case, Rachel and I were pleased with the appointment.

By mid-August, 1946, we were on our way to Valdosta with our one-month-old daughter wedged between us in a bassinet. We were in a 1941 Oldsmobile that had been run to death by some bigwig during WWII, but it was all we could get. Every now and then, the hood would fly up, requiring a stop on the shoulder of Highway 41 to slam it shut again. The speedometer didn't work, so we never knew how fast we were going! At least the brakes worked, and we stopped for the one-light towns along the way. But we knew we were blessed. I had a job, and we were on our way to making a life together.

Housing was scarce in Valdosta, as it was everywhere. That postwar song "My heart gets sore when I read on the door, No Vacancy" was on every radio. However, my immediate superior at the college, already on the scene, had arranged for the three of us to rent a room in a home on North Toombs Street. We went immediately to the designated house and found that the room was small for two adults and a baby, but we "hung in there" until larger quarters became available. It was difficult amid complaints that our baby was crying too loudly!

The next day, I went to work and, at first, was mistaken for a student! The Registrar tried to register me for the Fall Quarter. I declined, explaining that I was there to teach his Western Civilizations classes. He looked surprised. Nearly every student there was a veteran recently released from some branch of the armed forces, so I looked, and was, about their same age. In the meantime, Rachel was back at the room trying to keep our baby quiet. Her nerves were frayed by the time I got back that evening, so I moved about with great care to avoid an India-style earthquake. We persevered there for over a year.

All was not bad. Being lifelong Methodists, we immediately joined the Valdosta First Methodist Church. During my Army years, I had become somewhat skeptical about a number of religious concepts, but Rachel was steadfast, so we moved together in harmony in trying to establish our family in worthwhile causes, including the Church as a base. Soon we were active in all phases of Church work and other civic efforts. In those efforts, we met some of the finest people in the world.

Rachel soon commandeered the dilapidated Oldsmobile that had no working speedometer! I rode with her one day and noted that the telephone and power poles were speeding by at a questionable rate. We thanked God she had not been stopped by the police and went at once to the "Oldsmobile place," where the problem was repaired at a price of eighteen dollars. Our first Thanksgiving was marred by a wreck. We had been to the city library, and on the way home I misjudged the speed of an oncoming taxi, pulling straight in front of it and getting slammed, on Rachel's side! She was somewhat nonplused, but unhurt. Next day, we took both cars to a repair shop for appraisal of damages, which came to a total of five hundred dollars. The repairman refused to let us pay in installments. I told him to go ahead and repair both cars. I would be responsible.

Disaster loomed. We didn't have a cent, and the bill would be due in a few days. To top it all, the taxi driver sent a policeman to my office the next morning to arrest me because I had not "given satisfaction." I assured him I would pay when the cars were repaired. He went back to his car, talked to the taxi driver, then came back to tell me I would pay, or else. Or else! Oh Zeus! Rachel was distressed. I went to banks next day and begged for a loan. They all turned me down flat. Somebody prayed for us, I think, for when I got back to my office, a fellow faculty member, Dan Moore, was waiting for me with a check for five hundred dollars. I offered to sign a note to assure him I would pay the money back with interest. He refused, saying he had just retired as an officer in the Army and had enough to let me have the money as long as I needed it. "Touched by an Angel." Rachel and I wept. I borrowed money from my Army insurance policy and repaid the debt, but that process took about two months. Had it not been for Dan, we supposed that "or else" would have taken over.

Our circle of friends in Valdosta continued to grow. Their hospitality was overwhelming, their genuine good will heartwarming. We decided this was the place we would settle for the duration of our lives. One couple offered to teach us to play bridge. They came to our apartment full of bridge and anxious to teach us the splendor of the game. The game began amicably—looked as if Rachel and I might like it. But very soon, one guest told us to do one thing, the other said "No, you are telling them wrong." They argued for a few seconds, slammed down the cards, hardly bade us good evening, and went home never to return! We decided, Rachel and I, that we didn't wish to play a game for blood, so we settled for canasta.

We took many trips together to such places as the developing Jekyll Island, and other islands on the Georgia coast. Bishop Arthur Moore was pushing hard at that time to establish Epworth-by-the-Sea, a Methodist retreat facility, at Jekyll Island. We spent a little time there, but the place was too rugged for pleasure trips. It was only a short distance from Valdosta to Waycross and the Okefenokee Swamp entrance. Also, Florida was close by. Our first vacation was to Ellinor Village, near St. Augustine, I think.

We did all we could to enjoy life together while fulfilling our responsibilities in Valdosta. Once when we were going to the Georgia coast, the college dietitian begged to keep our "sweet little daughter" during the time we were to be away. We hesitated about leaving our baby with someone else but finally agreed. When we returned after the weekend trip, it turned out that our "sweet little daughter" had created bitterness in the dietitian's heart. She hit us with a broadside of complaints, all felonies. After that, our daughter went with us on such occasions, sweet or not!

Episodes in the Life of a Bumpkin

It came to pass that friction developed between the college Dean and the dietitian. The dietitian wanted to require students to wear coats and ties to Sunday lunch in the college dining room. War weary veterans thought that was *bleep* and petitioned the dean, who agreed and ordered the dietitian to cease and desist. Since the dean was the boss, she had to go, amidst fur flying far and near. The parting was somewhat less than amicable. Since Rachel had taken home economics courses at Reinhardt College, the dean sent for her to come in for an interview. He deemed her qualified to be College dietitian and appointed her to the position. She retained the position for the remaining six years we were there. We then moved into the Main Dormitory Proctor's apartment, and, in addition to my other duties, I became Proctor! Our "sweet little daughter" was with us, of course! She once created quite a sensation among the students when she appeared in the dining room and hopped up on the windowsill sans clothing. Rachel, hearing the commotion, rushed to the aid of decorum and re-clothed the subject of the illegal demonstration.

I found that the proctor's job could involve some anxious moments. It seems that the town boys considered the "Emily" Junior boys to be pantywaists, lace on their drawers, etc. Sometimes this would cause resentment and friction between the two groups. One night, I heard about four cars roar in and go to the back of the dormitory. As the cars emptied, their occupants could be heard running up the back stairs. There was great commotion up there, and I didn't even have a gun, much less three bullets. I called city Police. They came forty minutes later, and by that time the matter upstairs had been settled and the cars had roared away. Looked to me like the police were as big cowards as I was!

Another incident was much more serious. A student knocked frantically at our apartment one night and implored me to follow him to his room. I asked to know what was wrong. He said, "Just come, and please hurry." When we arrived at his door, I saw that he had a chair outside it. He wanted me to stand in that chair and look in through the transom. He had come in from somewhere and found his roommate hanging from their high upper bunk. He was choking himself to death for his rope stretched and his feet dragged the floor. We cut him down and sent him to the hospital. He later transferred to Georgia Tech and was said to be making an A in all subjects!

The whole town was shocked when, in late spring 1948, the very popular J. B. Harrington, Registrar of the College, died of a heart attack. The Dean (chief executive of the college) immediately appointed me to serve with him on a committee of two to find a new registrar! Rachel and I helped entertain numerous candidates during the summer. Each candidate was offered the position, but all declined. Plans for fall registration must be made in the very near future, and the Dean had him no second in command, a registrar, to get the job done. The unthinkable happened. He walked into my office announcing, "Cox, I am appointing you Registrar of the College." I tried to get him to see that I was not interested in administration, that I came to teach history. He didn't hear a word I said. As he walked briskly down the hall, hopping because, he said, his brother had once stuck a pitchfork in his foot (the Dean's foot, not his brother's), words trailed behind him to the effect that he would appoint me an assistant. The proposed assistant would have none of it. He was more persuasive than I, but he is now deceased.

So, for the remaining five years of our sojourn there, Rachel was Dietitian, and I was Registrar, in addition to my duties in the history classroom. We soon were rid of the errant Oldsmobile and in a new Hudson Hornet! It served us well in long trips to visit mine and Rachel's parents, as well as on shorter pleasure trips. We bought a little house to begin our long life in Valdosta. We continued our church and community work and were happy.

We had made a momentous decision. We would be a one-child family! Lillian was five when Vivian was born in 1951. Vivian was almost two when Linton III (Lin) was born in 1953. If fate hadn't moved us from Valdosta, no telling how many we would have had! We decided that the Valdosta water must be unusually potent. I thought when Lillian was born that I knew all there was to know about raising children.

By the time Linton came along, I knew that I didn't know a thing about it. Rachel was better educated than I. Her teaching was mingled with just the right amount of discipline to raise balanced children. She had had experience teaching in elementary schools, and, as the ninth of ten siblings, she had contributed much to the raising of numerous nieces and nephews.

Vivian required much attention during her early months. She was under normal weight at birth and required feeding every two hours. Rachel could not stand that, day and night, so I did the night feeding. Together, we pulled Vivian through the anxious months and years. In the meantime, Lillian entered school in 1952. Her teacher quickly found that she had serious eye problems. We immediately began efforts to get the problem under control. Lillian has worn glasses continuously since that time.

Our years in Valdosta were cut off due to problems we didn't anticipate but should have. Our enrollment during the first few years was ninety percent veterans, and when they graduated and moved on, we didn't have the power as a "junior" college to attract hordes of high school graduates. Enrollment dwindled to the point that Emory, for financial reasons, was forced to close the college permanently in 1953. I was offered a job on Emory's Atlanta campus. (For a complete history of Emory-At-Valdosta's twenty-one years of operation, see Cox and Lawrence, *Pride and Abandonment, The Story of Emory-At-Valdosta, 1928-1953,* Boyd Publishing Company, 2000.)

EMORY UNIVERSITY

In late summer 1953, we loaded ourselves, our three babies, some of our belongings, and three large watermelons into the big Hudson we had bought and struck out for Decatur. We were on our way to a little house on Medlock Road (later renamed Woodridge). I had signed on for the house without Rachel ever seeing it! I held my breath until she had inspected every room and every inch of the yard and given me the nod of approval. We had a good laugh. I entered my work at Emory. Within a few months, she was keeping neighborhood children for working parents to help with expenses.

While we lived on Medlock/Woodridge Road, Linton III (Lin) decided there were "woofies" in the attic. I don't know where he got that name, but he was worried about his woofies and wanted to see them. Access to the attic was in the carport, so I borrowed a ladder from a neighbor and walked closely behind Lin as he struggled to climb to the opening. He watched impatiently as I removed the cover to the opening, then put his head up where he could look all around. He inspected the attic in disappointment, but that satisfied his curiosity, and he forgot about his woofies.

Also, while there, Rachel and I went to the pound and acquired a dog. Lin bit him on the nose, and he bit Lin back. Bedlam ensued, leading us to conclude that a live dog was a bad idea for our family at that time. However, when one of my Emory friends, Luke Clegg, who lived out on Cocklebur Road, found out about our decision, he brought our kids one of his dogs! Lin did not bite it.

Our daughter, Evelyn, was born August 24, 1954. Luke Clegg volunteered to take me aside soon and explain to me what caused babies. I think Rachel already knew! We decided we could support no more adequately. We stuck to the decision this time! When my wonderful mother-in-law found out about the pregnancy, she came into her living room where several of us were sitting and shook her fist in my face. I sent one of Rachel's sisters in the kitchen to tell her she was visiting in our home, asleep, when the initial stage took place and, if she objected, should have stayed alert enough to stop the action. Uproarious laughter was heard from the kitchen.

Facetiously, I ordered Rachel not to have Evelyn in the middle of the night. I needed my rest! Just to spite me, Evelyn was born August 24. 1954—at about three in the morning. That proves that I was a mean, overbearing husband and that such a miscreant cannot always have his way. She said I was not required to go to the hospital! Which reminds me of a young sailor who asked for a furlough to be present when his child was born, and was told, "Son, it was necessary for you to be there at the laying of the keel but it is not necessary for you to be present at the launching." I think I have digressed again. I should get rid of that habit.

If the above suggests that Rachel was pregnant with Evelyn at the time of this story, she was. About mid-afternoon on August 23, she had the first contraction. Rachel was slow to reach the point of birth with all of our children, and Evelyn was slower to decide to face the world than any of the rest. I projected in my mind that with a mid-afternoon first contraction the baby would appear at about ten post meridian and suggested that I take Rachel on to the hospital just in case.

But Rachel wanted a freezer. She asked that we go to Sears, Roebuck so she could choose one. She wanted to go right now. Sears was about five miles away on Ponce de Leon, across the street from the Atlanta Crackers' baseball field. The Sears building later became Atlanta City Hall East, and the stadium went up in the smoke of the Atlanta Braves.

As I said, Rachel wanted a freezer. We had some vegetables Dad had brought to us from his garden. They needed freezing because she was unable to can them, she said. I could see that she was unable to stand over a hot stove, but I felt sure the freezing could wait another day or so. I argued. I should have had better sense, so, of course, we started to Sears. I quipped all the way there and that was another mistake. I feared that our fourth child would be born in a *bleeped* freezer. I suggested further that we might want to name our fourth child Sears Cox. She was negatively impressed. We negotiated and purchased a freezer. Rachel persuaded the Sears delivery folks to deliver it that very afternoon! We rushed back home, for I had to get the closet at the end of the carport cleaned out; that being one and the same carport from which Evelyn later ran away from home because I would not let her throw my nails all over the yard. The carport closet was the only place in our small house to put a twenty-foot freezer. All that was done, the freezer installed, the vegetables placed therein, and we collapsed for the night. The contractions were getting closer together, but Rachel kept putting off going to the hospital. She told me to go to sleep.

About two or two-thirty in the morning, she called upon me to arise and transport her to the hospital without delay. Now, I could imagine a stop on the way, on the side of the road, with a confused history major beating his head on the hood of the car, and Rachel yelling at him to DO SOMETHING. He would have, but the baby was still in place when we got to the hospital unloading zone, and the doctor was waiting. Something, at least, was going my way.

Evelyn was born, and I was allowed in to see Rachel. She was furious. The doctor didn't think the birth was imminent and was in another part of the hospital when the moment of reality came. The nurses took care of the birth. Rachel demanded that I look the doctor up and beat his *bleep*. Actually, she was quite graphic in her instructions. I told her to please calm down, that I would take care of the matter at once. A nurse followed me into the hallway and assured me the birth went well, that the doctor was there to make his usual examination on time. Good! I hadn't planned to beat his *bleep* anyway. But, all this just goes to show what troubles a husband can create for himself.

Evelyn was born with a problem, related to Bright's disease, which required surgery at age four. The surgeon, Dr. Hamm, at Piedmont Hospital, performed the surgery. Evelyn accused Rachel and me of trying to have her killed! Later, after similar surgery, her daughter accused Evelyn of the same murderous intent.

We joined North Decatur Methodist Church, which at that time was only a basement. We made many friends there. I made at least one enemy.

We needed more space to accommodate four children, so about 1956 we traded our house on Woodridge for one on North Decatur Road near Emory. That house had bedrooms upstairs and a garage in the basement, so we were adequately served until 1960, when I accepted a position at Alabama College in Montevallo, and we moved. The house sold quickly. I nailed a sign to a tree in the front yard early on a Saturday morning. At two o'clock that afternoon, a contractor was knocking at the door! I told him Rachel was running a birthday party in the house, which she was, and that he might want to postpone his inspection of the house until Monday. He said "naw," he had grandchildren and he would not bother them, or *vice-versa*. He wanted to buy the house. Being unversed in the art of salesmanship, I pointed out every flaw in the house that I knew about! He reminded me that he was a contractor and could fix every one of them without difficulty. Before I could collect my wits, he was peeling off hundred-dollar bills as earnest money. I hesitated to take the money, assuring him I would consider the house sold to him. He insisted. He would see me Monday to sign the papers! I met him at a bank, and we closed the deal. He gave me one hundred dollars more than we had asked for the house, because, he said, he loved to deal with honest men. As far as I know, his middle name was not Diogenes.

Our oldest child, Lillian, was broken-hearted over leaving Atlanta. She had ridden ponies at a little farm on Briarcliff Road for several years and feared nothing like that would be available in Alabama. Rachel and I were saddened by her grief, but it was time to make a change at the adult level. All four were curious about what Alabama would be like. Where was Alabama? How close to Atlanta would we be? Would they have any friends there? So, I concocted some wild stories, in which Rachel backed me up. The first one was that a great ditch separated us from them, and that when we moved, we would need to run the car as fast as we could to jump the ditch. They told that all over their schools and anywhere else they could get an audience! When we started the journey, I told them to watch for Tallapoosa, and from there to watch closely for "Alabama" signs. The old Chevy coupe was electrified with excitement as they watched for the ditch, and when it did not materialize, I was surely glad they didn't have guns. Ahhh Daddy!!

I took Rachel and the children on to Montevallo and helped them get settled in a rented house that belonged to Alabama College. I then returned to Emory to complete my contract that ended the last of August. As I entered the car for the return trip, I leaned over the back of the front seat too swiftly and broke two ribs. Luckily, there are more ways than one to turn over in the bed. I found one of them. My contract completed, I cleaned out my desk and prepared to return to Alabama. Friends appeared with a set of golf clubs and advised me to learn to use them, because Alabama College had a golf course. I went to the driving range one time, dug up the ground and lost my ball, and never went back again.

REFLECTIONS

THAT TRIP FROM THE EMORY Administration Building down to my car, golf clubs swung on my shoulder, was one of the longest I have ever taken. I could not control my emotions and let the tears roll. Grown men don't cry, they say. I didn't cry. I just bellowed. Finally, my control returned, I pulled out into North Decatur Road on my way to Lullwater and Ponce de Leon and points west, nevermore to be connected to Emory in any official capacity. I reflected—on how I got there, and the intervening years.

I got there through the services of Rev. T. Newton Wise, Pastor at Mt. Gilead Methodist. Shortly after I graduated from Reinhardt, Newton talked with Dad, who agreed that I should go to Emory. Newton set a date for us to see J. Gordon Stipe, who controlled admissions at that time. Mr. Stipe looked at my Reinhardt transcript carefully and deemed me qualified for admission. Then Newton took me to the Emory Cafeteria, where I was interviewed by Mrs. Haynie, University Dietitian and a truly great lady. She hired me. So, all was set for my matriculation in fall quarter, 1940.

Mother was disturbed, and that caused me some anguish. She was so thoroughly convinced that the Emory Theology School faculty was perverting the gospel and had surrendered to Satan that she was just sure my young mind was too immature to sort out the truth. She appeared to beckon me back to her side of Polecat Mountain. Dad probably had some of the same fears, but he didn't voice them. Grandmother did voice her doubts that the right school for me was Emory. Maybe Asbury or a similar institution would be better for me. Dad remained firm in his silence. He took me to register at Emory at the appointed time, as he had taken me across Polecat Mountain to Reinhardt.

Mother pondered all those things in her heart until Christmas of that first year. Under the Christmas tree for me that year was an *Authorized King James Version of the Bible* with this inscription, "Proverbs I: 10" which reads: "My son, if sinners entice thee, consent thou not." If I saw that quotation for the first time today, I would steal a ploy from a former U. S. President and say, "define sinners."

A number of people hinted to me that they were afraid I might be a bit unstable, vulnerable, and weak in my faith. A theology student who had graduated a couple of years ahead of me at Reinhardt looked me up very soon after I enrolled in Fall 1940 to tell me to be careful, that my faith of yesteryear would certainly be assailed from every direction.

I drove westward toward Alabama and thought of all the Emory folks who had helped to the point of my departure. I mention names with caution, because some great person of influence will certainly be inadvertently overlooked. I will mention some of the most important anyway. Others who helped need not feel slighted, for I am old.

E. D. Whisonant at Valdosta took me under his wing immediately. A young whippersnapper just out of the Army, feeling his oats, met a seasoned veteran of the wars of education. He assessed my weak spots as he saw them and sought to apply his wisdom as an improvement medium. Much of that wisdom brought me face to face with areas of life I had never entered, and really had no thought of entering. Possibly, he saw my religious faith as wobbly! I'm sure he did! As a junior member of the administration of a Methodist sponsored college, I should act like one. Within the first month of my tenure, he had scheduled me to speak at the eleven o'clock service of two Methodist Churches, Attapulgus and Abbeville. Now, that scared me silly, but he didn't ask me. He just told me. I built me a couple of "sermons" quoting every book in the Bible and then some, wrote them out, and read every word I had written. I may also have read a few lines from Boccacio's *Decameron* and Chaucer's *Canterbury Tales*. I don't know. I wasn't responsible. I made sure they realized that Dean Whisonant sent me!

I guess I didn't completely ruin Methodism. Soon, he had me speaking at churches all over the South Georgia Conference, at commencements, and at whatever other organizations he could find. One would have thought I was much in demand! Horse feathers! But a Methodist horse, Sir. I got some good meals at lunch after the service, and some that suggested I was being punished for doing a poor job. I lied about the quality of some foods proffered me. The best I ever ate, etc. Zeus!

When the Valdosta unit of Emory closed, there was a man in the office of the College of Arts and Sciences on the Atlanta campus who asked for me. He was H. Prentice Miller, Dean of the College's Lower Division. He was joined by Judson C. Ward, Jr.,

Dean of the entire College, in welcoming me as Assistant Dean of the College. As some moderns might express it, I was pumped. I was humbly grateful that I should be so recognized without asking for the position. I could never have worked for two more wonderful men than Miller and Ward. It speaks to their greatness that the relatively new Alumni House bears their names. I went to a reception there not long ago, and, since I had forgotten my belt and left it in Milledgeville, my pants fell off. I shall be known as the only alumnus in history who ever mooned the crowd in a building that bears the names of two such wonderful men. My daughter, Vivian, who drove me up there, thought the event of my loss to be very funny. God, help me!

One of my very best friends in the Emory University Administration was Lewis Lamar (Luke) Clegg, University Director of Admissions. He was a wise, perceptive and witty colleague. When I would fear to leave my office for a break with work on my desk, Luke would come to my door and beckon me out to go to the Majestic Café for an hour of coffee, doughnuts and hamburgers. Nobody ever questioned Luke about his interrupting my official schedule. He, Charlie Watson, Director of Financial Aid, and I, sometimes adding Howard Phillips, Dean of the Graduate School, would take off to the Majestic. We would also often have lunch together at Mary Mac's downtown on Ponce de Leon. Now and then, Sam Shiver, Professor of German, would join us and tell some of his ribald stories. I had best not repeat any of them here. Oh, just one, a one-liner. He said the German word for brassiere is holtzumfumfloppen.

So, had I run across those awful sinners at Emory? I majored in history, and those professors on the top floor of the Law Building sort of let my faith drift about as it would—and taught me history. I took only one course from a School of Theology professor, Dr.

Arva Floyd. That course was the "History of the Far East," and I suppose ir might be considered sinful, since it mentioned some other religions over there. "From all the dark places of earth's needy races, Oh see how the thick shadows fly! The voice of salvation awakes every nation, 'Come over and help us they cry.'" Obviously, they weren't wide awake and calling us very loudly as they murdered our missionaries. Lest I rattle on, let me mention one of my history professors, James Harvey Young, a great scholar and a cherished friend.

Harvey was a true friend of his majors. He and his wife, Myrna, often visited Rachel and me in our home, whether it be our little war-surplus trailer on the Emory campus, or our dormitory apartment at Emory-At-Valdosta, or our nine-room house in Milledgeville. That has been a grand association through the years. Rachel and Myrna are now dead. Harvey and I are fading, but still correspond. He was a great teacher, taking his students where they were and nudging them to higher levels of understanding. Whatever he was, he was and is not a sinner. He was and is a man of the Love of God, although he would never claim that distinction.

Greatest in influence on my decision to leave Emory was Dr. Goodrich C. White, President of the University. He probably wanted me to advance in stature, but not necessarily at Emory. I have to assume that his strange methods of dealing with me were not motivated by personal animosity. He was a stalwart man of great dignity. He could be brutally decisive at times, as the time he fired two Medical School faculty members for going to the newspapers with their complaints. Usually, his actions were milder. I had no direct access to him and did nothing to aggravate him through Dean Miller or Dean Ward. Yet, I had the uneasy feeling that he wanted me to leave Emory.

His first indication came when he met me in the hallway one day and stopped me to talk, in itself an unusual event. He asked me whether I was looking for a job elsewhere. I replied in the negative. Then he let me have what was on his mind. "Well, you should be looking," he stated. "You are in a dead-end job here." I knew he wasn't speaking of a portion of my anatomy, rather of my professional advancement. Later, I tried to think of anything I might have done to displease him, and could remember none, except maybe the time I tracked dog doo into his thickly carpeted living room. He had invited Valdosta Dean Whisonant and me to meet him in his home for a conference. I walked up the driveway directly behind the Dean and never could figure out why he didn't step in that stuff instead of me. It fell to my lot to get a good supply of the doo on the bottom of my shoe, and I placed about six contaminated markings in his carpet. Oh. Lord! Oh well, it was his dog that had so little couth as to put it on the walkway!

Shortly, I found myself getting inquiries from small Methodist colleges as to whether I would come for an interview. Apparently, my President was putting out the message that I might be available. One was from the President of Lambuth College in Jackson, Tennessee. The position would have been all right, but the President wanted me to commit as to whether I would accept a job if he offered one to me. I could not do that. A job offer would have had to be specific and discussed with my family before I could respond. I didn't want to leave Emory and probably would have rejected an offer.

Among others was a call really late at night from the President of Hamline University in St. Paul, Minnesota, but I respectfully declined that interview. He said outright that President White had recommended me. That was probably a first-rate position, but I had frozen half to death south of his University down at Chanute Field, Illinois, and I was not about to drag my family that far north. I fiendishly hoped that Dr. White was awakened that night to learn of my action, just as I had been to receive the call.

A friend in Macon, Georgia approached me about applying for the presidency of Wesleyan College. That invitation did not come at the behest of Dr. White, who was Chairman of the selection committee! I had made no move at all on that suggestion, but Dr. White, for the first and last time ever, came to my office. He said, "I understand you are interested in the Wesleyan presidency." I told him I had been asked to apply but was not likely to let it go any further than that. "Good, we are looking for someone who is qualified," he said. He is now deceased.

So, it looked as if I should go. I had all the support I needed from Dean Miller and Dean William C. Archie, new Dean of the College. Dean Ward had become Academic Vice-President. Later, Dean Archie offered to match the salary Howard Phillips had offered me at Alabama College, if I would stay at Emory. But that would look like I had sought the Alabama offer to prize for a higher salary at Emory! Many others engaged in that kind of approach. Why didn't I? Because I didn't want to. Emory would pay me more money when it became available and when I was considered worthy of it. I was not only a jerk. I was a naïve jerk! Dr. White had by that time retired and been succeeded by Dr. S. Walter Martin, who was to play a key role in my life later on. Later, I was honored to be appointed by the then Governor of District 6920 of Rotary International to write Dr. Martin's obituary. I could, from my own knowledge, speak to his greatness.

MONTEVALLO

By the time I got to Talladega, I was in Alabama and on my way to a new challenge. So, I quit reflecting on where I had been. It was time for a forward march. I was far, far away from Polecat Mountain but the effects of the crossing lingered.

Friends were as easy to make in Montevallo, Alabama as they had been anywhere else, and the children soon realized that. Lillian was soon riding horses on a farm nearby, owned by the President's secretary and her husband. Vivian, Linton III, and Evelyn fell right in with their age groups. Rachel soon became an assistant in the college library, and I assumed my duties as Director of Admissions and Recruitment. We joined the Methodist Church and entered into other community activities. Some mighty fine, down-to-earth people lived around there. I threatened to divorce Rachel and engineer the divorce of another couple who lived over in Pea Ridge. I would then marry that lady who made the best fig preserves this side of Mt. Olympus! Lordy, those preserves were the best I had ever tasted. My plans didn't work. The lady kept us supplied with jars of her delicacy, and all the maneuvering I had thought up vanished. I could not tell whether Rachel was sad or glad!

We made several weekend trips back to Georgia while we lived in Montevallo. The most memorable are the ones we made to Chatsworth. Lin was always hungry before we got out of Montevallo. He knew what was in the cooler and began to ask when we would stop to eat. Our stopping place was a small picnic area on the side of what may have been Sand Mountain. Anyway, it was before we got to Talladega and on to Oxford. From there it was clear sailing on through Calhoun and Spring Place, Georgia to Chatsworth. Back to the roadside picnic area—our dog, Lady, loved to rest there. Lady often *bleeped* there while the children ate.

At first, on those trips we stayed with Rachel's Mother. But it was a small house and adding six people to an already crowded house was just too much. On weekends, several of "Mama Gregory's" ten children and a host of grandchildren were there for a visit. Rachel and I switched to a motel about a mile away, called "The Pines." That hurt some feelings among the ten siblings and Rachel, but we had to do it to keep from imposing unmercifully in the Gregory home. Incidentally, there was a restaurant across the road from the motel where, in the Depression days, Rachel had bought me a T-bone steak, complete with french fries and a vegetable, for only ninety cents.

The motel worked well for our children. A large corner room that we always called several days in advance to reserve had three queen size beds, adequate to sleep our family of six comfortably. The main attraction there was a swimming pool, and the children thought that to be so "hunky dory," they named the motel "High Heaven." In plain view of Fort Mountain, it was pretty near Heaven.

Generally, our days in Montevallo were relatively pleasant, though we did have some internal family problems that shook us up a bit. Also, I learned some things about my President that I had not noted at Emory when we worked side by side there. He could be rough on his friends as well as those he considered to be his enemies. I learned too that one had best not hitch his professional wagon to any one person. Within two years, he had agreed to become President of Birmingham Southern College. Although I had a good relationship with the faculty and other administrators, and Rachel was surviving the storm of budget cuts that threatened her job, George Wallace was a threat to everybody in government service. Rachel and I decided we must seek refuge back in familiar territory. I put out the word with my friends back in Georgia. I told my friend J. Edward Hall, a friend and a recruiter for Emory, and he spread the word on campus to folks like Clegg and Watson, Miller and Ward, Archie, and others. Somebody told Dr. Walter Martin, then Vice-Chancellor of the University System of Georgia. He knew where positions were open in the System. In fact, he knew of one position that had been declined by one or more of my Emory friends who were helping me find a job! That worked to my advantage.

MILLEDGEVILLE

SOON I RECEIVED A CALL from the Woman's College of Georgia in Milledgeville. It was President Robert E. Lee (not that one), inviting me to come for interviews. I was more than pleased to get the call, and Rachel sighed in relief. I appeared for the interviews, conducted by the President and other College officials, and was hired. When Dr. Lee took me to introduce me to Dr. T. E. Smith, the man I was to replace, Dr. Smith raised his hands toward heaven and said "Oh, Good! We were getting desperate around here." They just didn't know how desperate! Rachel and I began to prepare our belongings and our children for return to Georgia, and did so for the fall quarter, 1963.

Rachel immediately secured a position as a substitute teacher in the Baldwin County Schools, and I began my duties as Registrar and Director of Admissions at The Woman's College. We had moved into a rented home, owned by a lady who was out of the country for a year. She left Charlie, her dog, in our care. Charlie didn't like me and tore up my right hand to prove his point. He had torn up a neighbor's elbow the previous year. I went to the hospital to get my hand repaired but was replaced in the emergency room by a young woman whose husband had pumped a bullet through her head. He stood in the hallway and prayed loudly that God would not let her die! She died.

We started unpacking just as President Lee rolled into our driveway and told me to pack at once. We had a meeting in Young Harris, Georgia. Poor Rachel was left to unpack and take care of four children. She didn't complain. We were too happy to be here. When we returned, I went to work and inquired as to the location of my office. Dr. Smith looked surprised and said he didn't know. I rattled around for several days while Herb Meyer, Comptroller, walled me off a little cubbyhole in an already crowded space. Since I had faced a similar situation upon my arrival in Montevallo, it didn't bother me. It did tell me that my appointment did not stir up much interest on either campus, and that I was not expected to ride into town on a donkey with palm branches flying and crowds shouting Hosanna!

In 1964, we bought a home on North Columbia Street, one block from the college, and that site was to remain our home for thirty years. It had nine rooms and was adequate for raising our four children. Also, it was handy for me to walk to my work so Rachel could have a car to consider her own in her positions in the prison system, in adult education, and in the Foster Grandparent/Senior Companion programs.

Amidst all our busy schedule, we managed to eat as a family of six around the large round oak table we had bought in North Georgia for three dollars! Around that table, we laughed, joked, and solved problems to the best of our ability. We often grilled steaks, hot dogs, or whatever we might be able to afford. In some months there was much month left over at the end of the money. Often, I crawled to the bank and begged for a loan. I was always received cordially and got the loan. Getting up the courage to ask was the hardest part. A husband and wife who had grown up as children of the Great Depression wanted fervently to live within our income. We sometimes couldn't, and also give the children the privileges they deserved.

When I had business trips, I always invited Rachel to go with me, and she always declined on the bases of her job and the necessity for one of us to be with our "babies." Then one day, as we sat around the round oak table for supper, I mentioned my next trip and invited Rachel as usual. When she mentioned our "babies," our youngest, then seventeen, emphatically informed Rachel that she had no babies. That shocked Rachel into accepting my invitation! The trip was to St. Louis for a three- or four-day conference. We borrowed daughter Lillian's Chevy van, stuffed it with the necessities accompanying a trip of that distance, and entered into a new phase of our marriage, in which we could go places together. We took two weekends, one on either side of the conference, so that our jobs would not suffer, except for the absence of our scintillating presence among our cohorts.

We drove through Tennessee, and made reservations at a Holiday Inn in Mt. Vernon, Illinois for the second night. As we entered southern Illinois, I handed Rachel the road map and asked her to keep me on the path to Mt. Vernon. I forgot to mention there is also a Mt. Vernon in Indiana! She got me nearly there before I realized that something was amiss. We then had a hearty laugh, turned around, and headed for the right Mt. Vernon. Next day, we traveled on to St. Louis, which was in pretty much of a shambles in the early seventies. We had made our reservations there late and had to take a room in a run-down motel that was surrounded by a high wire fence. We wondered whether we could get out when the conference was over. But we had a great time.

During the seventies, we had other trips to college-related meetings. After St. Louis, we saw such places as Cleveland, Ohio; New Orleans, Louisiana; Miami, Florida; and Atlanta. Perhaps the most memorable was San Francisco, where my national meeting was held in 1981. I had a position in the Association and was given a small stipend for editing the national Newsletter. I used the stipend for our travel expenses, thus sparing the parsimonious travel budget of my office. Rachel had never flown, so I thought she should have that trip in a transcontinental flight. I got round trip tickets on Delta, First Class, and prayed the journey would be "ceiling and visibility unlimited" (CAVU) coast to coast. It was, both ways. Rachel was sold on flying! I think she would have wanted to go by air if our meeting had been in Devereux, a few miles east toward Sparta, Georgia!

On the return flight, we were treated to a champagne breakfast. Oh Boy! This old country couple had never seen such luxury. When we landed in Atlanta, we went to the motel and slept a while! There was no hurry to get back to Milledgeville.

One bonus for Rachel was that side excursions were planned for those not directly involved in the conference sessions. As editor of the Newsletter, I had to be about my Association's business, but she could take those side trips into the countryside, and she thoroughly enjoyed doing that. One drawback was that one of our neighbors considered it her responsibility to relate every move each of our four children had taken in our absence—"just thought you would want to know," said she. Coming home late at night was one of the items upon which she had complete information. Finally, I had had enough of it, and I took over from Rachel who usually caught all the flak. The lady reporter made much of the fact that one of the four came in one night at 3:00 A. M. When she assailed me with that astounding piece of information, I informed her that I was absolutely certain the accused always came in between nine and ten. She was dumbfounded. That was my story and I stuck to it. I had named one of the porch posts nine, and the opposite one ten. We got no more reports from that news organization.

One of our journeys was to Houston, Texas. Before that meeting was over, I was about ready to call our son and ask him to fly to Texas and drive us back home. My back was out. The story of why my back was out is almost too tragic to relate. We had a nice room at the headquarters hotel, with all the necessary appointments for a comfortable stay, except that the two beds were quite narrow and uncomfortable, which has nothing to do with why my back was out.

You see, all my life I have had terrible nightmares, kicking and screaming, and swearing "like a sailor," although I served in the Army Air Force. We used unacceptable language there too. Anyway, I had one of those nightmares in Houston. Rachel's walking stick would not reach me from her bunk, so I had free wheeling. Of all things, I saw in my dream a dog over by the couch, a vicious looking animal baring his teeth and growling. At least that was what my twisted imagination told me he was doing. So, I walked over to the side of the couch and kicked that dog with mighty force. Let me tell you. That was the hardest dog I ever kicked. In fact, I had never in my life kicked a dog. We didn't have a dog in my pre-Polecat Mountain days, and the one Rachel and I had later in Milledgeville was not ours. It belonged to our children, so I never kicked it—just wanted to a few times. But, to my great chagrin, that Houston dog was solid wall. My big toe on my right foot felt as if I had driven it right through the wall. It was a terrible toe tragedy, and that's why my back was out. Lately, my left foot and ankle have been swelling, but not my right. Maybe I should have kicked the wall with both feet so they would match.

When in town, we continued our Church activities at First Methodist, as well as other community participation. My Emory classmate, Charlie Middlebrooks, was Pastor during our first years here. He was a bit of a rascal and played a few tricks on me in funds solicitation, sending me out to homes where he knew such solicitation was unwelcome. After I was bitten by dogs in two such places, I caught on and forever resigned from any church job which required me to go to a home to ask for pledges.

When I confronted Charlie with my decision, he grinned. When a future Pastor talked me into being Finance Chair, and I told the story at the home round table, Rachel led a chorus of raucous laughter. "YOU," Finance Chairman? HAW, HAW, HAW! I laughed too, but I later found out that I could handle other people's money much better than I could handle our own.

In the meantime, we were taking our children to regular Sunday morning services, and they and Rachel were participating in many of the Church programs. A few times, I did a mean thing. When I disagreed with some great theological point the Pastor had just made, I would write a note and pass it across our children to Rachel. As time passed, all four of the children could read! They would sneak a peek and express themselves in audible laughter. I had to stop that irreverent foolishness. If my Dad had known I did such a thing, I think he would have come to Milledgeville with a hickory switch and applied it warmly.

One of our means of family recreation was to go on one-day excursions to Jekyll Island. We would leave home about 4:00 a.m. and get to the Jekyll Island picnic area by 9:00 a.m. That would give the children a few hours of swimming time before eating the lunch Rachel had packed, and one or two more after we ate. Sometimes Rachel was in the water with them, but mostly she and I just watched closely. Rachel was an excellent swimmer and I a champion worrier. We would leave Jekyll late in the afternoon and be back home by bedtime.

Two fundamental changes in the nature of The Womans College of Georgia, to which I came, took place during my tenure—integration and coeducation. I had two understood mandates when I came to Milledgeville. They weren't written anywhere, but they were there, just understood. First, I would not agitate for co-education and second, I would not *bleep* up and admit a black student. I was to understand that this was a school for women, had always been and always would be. The convent would not be rent. The citadel would never be successfully assaulted. I was also to understand that segregated education was imbedded in society, represented by the Board of Regents. I accepted those terms, which might possibly be referred to as compromising with the economic devil, thus saving me from having to feed my family on polar bear meat.

I was not at the college long before the lid was blasted off. During my first year, I was visited by a number of leaders from the black community testing the waters as to my attitude toward the admission of black students. Since I was a minor player in the game, I was able to discuss my limitations with them within the context that rules must first be changed by Atlanta authorities before any move could be made in the direction they sought. They understood that, but wanted my attitude stated at least implicitly, since my office could employ all sorts of devious means to delay the admission process. I was careful not to express any breach between my attitude and that of the top administration, and yet to let them know that, given an order, immediate processing would be implemented.

The lid was blasted off. There was trouble at the University of Georgia, trouble at the University of Alabama, trouble all over. The hurricane was about to achieve category five status. The Legislature was on the hot seat. The Board of Regents in Atlanta was in turmoil. President Lee knew that I was "sitting on" several applications from black girls. A voice from the sky and from the person of President Lee came into my office in early 1964, closed the door, and said "Linton, I believe the time has come to consider applications from black girls." Society in general had not relented, but the Board of Regents had, and now we were free to begin the beginning of righting a tragic wrong.

By the time we got this clearance from above, we had only two applications from black girls left. The others had been cancelled by the applicants. One of the two applications left was from a student at Talladega College in Alabama who was applying for transient status for the summer quarter only. She came in summer of 1964 and returned to Talladega in the fall.

The other remaining applicant was a girl from Milledgeville with an excellent high school record and presentable SAT scores. She accepted our offer of admission. With no prompting from my office and, as far as I know, any other office of the College, she announced that she would be living at home. The Dean of Students was "off the hook." The applicant was then invited to come in for an interview, during which she was subjected to intensive questioning by top college officials as to whether she thought she could stand the pressure she might face. She underwent the interview well and graduated four years later. A person with less dignity than she had would have withered. Unfortunately, she found the going in the real world tougher than she might have anticipated. She was a real stalwart. A strong catalyst for change in a sea of prejudice that seems ever to be.

My concern now was to relate the action to the young ladies then enrolled, and to the old ladies who had graduated from the convent. That was not so difficult. They understood the tenor of the times pretty well. Some said it was all right, since she was a girl and living off campus! It was five years later when the Board of Regents for budgetary and pressure reasons decided the college must admit men. That was when the *bleep* hit the fan, and not all was spick and span. The convent was now rent in twain, ripped would be more like it. On recruiting trips, I was assailed, almost assaulted with questions as to why in the name of God Almighty did we have to admit boys, rendering the campus so fundamentally different from its historical purpose. Some pressed me to make a commitment that we would not have coed dorms! I had no power to make such a commitment and deferred that question to the Dean of Students! If asked the question today, I would say "define coed."

I put the official "spin" on the question of why the change of status was made by the Regents, that is, economic necessity. I put my own sentiments before them, pointing out that they were sending their daughters to the University of Georgia and not to their dear *Alma Mater*. They thought that was a heap of *bleep,* that I would have such audacity as to turn the tables on them!

THE FRUSTRATED FARMER

I INTERJECT HERE a very important aspect of our family life in Baldwin County, Georgia. First, I am a frustrated farmer. In spite of all the hardships of the Great Depression days, scratching out money from boll weevil infested cotton patches and food from soils depleted of their nutrients from bad farming practices, I wanted to farm. Plowing was recreation and renewal for me. I knew the productivity of the land could be restored. It seemed to me that tilling the soil was as close to God as anyone could get. He made the earth, and my reasoning suggested to me that He never made a city unless one counted the City of God that existed only in human imagination. God was in the fresh air, the rain, the aroma of new hay in the fall, the taste of fresh vegetables.

Short courses were available at the College of Agriculture in Athens. Rachel and I could go there on weekends for courses on soil building and protection, and food preservation. In other words, cooperation with God in His realm would pave the way for building an atmosphere somewhat akin to a Garden of Eden. When Rachel came into my life, we agreed that farming would play a key role in our romance. That was my dream throughout the war years, my hope, my faith that if I made it back home, Rachel and I would buy some acreage and build our lives there. Dad, discouraged by the Depression years, roughly 1928-1942, was no longer teaching school and was taking little jobs here and there. Maybe he would sell us some land. Otherwise, land would become available around there or near Chatsworth. The dreaming was good.

When WWII was over, Rachel and I began our lives in temporary residence with Dad and Mother. I began to cast my eyes about for available land. When I mentioned it, looks of horror always clouded Dad's face. "Son, you can't make a living farming," was his refrain. I was steadfast. If land became available near Chatsworth, as I was sure it would, that would put Rachel near her aging mother.

Something happened that changed my intended course of action. My discharge was issued in October, 1945. Around Thanksgiving 1945, I received a letter from Dr. Ross H. McLean, Chairman of the Department of History at Emory. He announced that my five-hundred-dollar fellowship, interrupted by the war, had been reactivated and urged me to accept. Faces other than mine lit up all over the house: those of Dad and Mother and, to my surprise, Rachel. Dad's refrain was repeated over and over, "Son, you can't make a living farming." Under tremendous pressure to accept the fellowship, I went to Emory and made arrangements for reentry in January 1946.

On the way home, reality hit me. What had I been doing? Whether I had any land or pursued other gainful employment, I couldn't raise a family in the Lickskillet District. It simply would not have worked. I was about to ruin Rachel's life and mine. At that point in time, I ceased to hope for land in Murray County. It was on to

Emory once more. The die was cast. I had crossed the Rubicon. As it did for Caesar centuries earlier, the Rubicon crossing refined me to a different reality, opening vistas here and closing some there. It added a new perspective to the Polecat Mountain crossing: reality.

Yet, land is soul for me, and I could not get it out of my mind that we might some day have some acres. In Valdosta, we had a large back yard. I fenced off the back thirty feet for a garden. That gave us fresh vegetables to eat and can. When Emory closed the Valdosta unit and we moved to Atlanta, with Rachel's permission and approval, I approached Dad about selling us some land. We would continue to live in Atlanta, I would do my job at Emory and drive the thirty miles to do a little farming on weekends. I don't know why I had so little sense. Fortunately, I feel, Dad wanted too much for his land, and that was that. He probably put the price up to a level he knew I wouldn't be financially able to reach. Anyway, living conditions would have been no better than before. Then we got on the other side of Polecat Mountain and approached "Mama Gregory," Rachel's Mother. She was willing to sell to us, but that was squelched by her brother who wanted the land for his children.

As I eyed land around Montevallo, Alabama, I thought briefly about pursuing a purchase there, but my job at the college kept me too busy, and I had to settle for fig preserves from our friends in Pea Ridge! But my passion for land followed me to Baldwin County, Georgia. I couldn't get rid of it—like a pesky song that gets re-played time after time on the storage tapes of the mind, whether wanted or not. I wanted land in mine and Rachel's name as owners. The song played for five years after we moved to Milledgeville with no action on the land matter. Then the volume increased. A friend who knew of this yearning referred us to Rev. James Ivey who was running a farm just east of town and wanted to sell a small portion of his land. We contacted him and picked out a twenty- acre site that fronted on Lake Laurel Road. We bought it in 1968, and it was a part of our family for a quarter century.

Rachel couldn't do farm work, but dearly loved to sit in the truck or in a chair and watch me and the children work! We understood. Our first job was to fence the property. A little fence existed already, but not much. Lillian, Vivian, Lin, Evelyn and I set about to get the job done. I bought wire cutters and stretchers, as well as fence posts, boots and raincoats. We worked rain or shine, weekends and holidays. We wanted to get the fencing done in a hurry, for animals were on our minds as inhabitants of the property.

Fencing done, we tackled building a barn with a feed room. I bought creosoted posts and secured them in the ground, brought in roofing and lumber, then backed off a bit and let the young folks build the barn around the posts. Our children brought in their friends to help. Such building of a barn one has never seen before and will never see again. When the finished structure took shape, the metal roof looked as if a contortionist had planned and erected a barn according to his most twisted pose. But, by golly, it didn't leak. The three large stables stayed dry except when floods sent waves of water down the hill. Even then, the feed room remained dry.

I looked around for a large garden plot and found two acres that we fenced off from the rest. The youngsters had learned to use the fence stretchers and to drive in staples. Again, they wanted to do the work, and I backed off. My garden came out much better in appearance than the barn roof!!

The first year we got under way, the place was pristine, with wild berries, quail, and small game. Kudzu abounded, probably initiated by CCC boys in the Roosevelt New Deal days as a conservation measure. We beat it back, sprayed it, whacked it, did all sorts of things to it, but it laughed at us. The only herbicide that would kill it, roots and all, was Agent Orange, and that was soon taken off the market.

That first summer, I picked fifteen gallons of blackberries. Rachel made jelly and jam, and some berries were frozen for pies. The weather was unusually favorable. I had several long rows of corn that produced in abundance. We canned and froze that and other vegetables. We grew all the basic vegetables: peas, green beans, okra, squash of several varieties, turnip greens and potatoes. The Reverend Ivey gave me some butternut squash seed that he must have blessed. They nearly took over my corn patch. We had all we could use, shared with others, and I took several bushels to camp Gwynn Valley, near Brevard, North Carolina, where our children were working. I gave the dietitian the several baskets of squash. I learned later that she served them as apples. The campers would have nothing to do with anything called squash, but they certainly went for those "apples."

My farming continued to be confined to my two acres. Lillian soon brought in several horses and I added several cows. We had to buy a great amount of feed. Twenty acres minus two could not maintain enough grasses for the number of animals we had there. Half the acreage was in woodland! I stuck to my gardening. My dream was realized. I could get out in God's country where He was. We got along as I had dreamed we would.

Rachel was happy with the arrangement. I brought home the vegetables. We processed them, often well into the morning hours.

Episodes in the Life of a Bumpkin

Then we went to our paying jobs. The children pursued whatever their interests in land were. Rachel "worked for an age at a sitting and never got tired at all." Thanks to Kipling.

I must confess there were times for concern. So-called "Cherokee Roses" were everywhere in the first years. They were coarse and thorny and just a general nuisance to have growing in good soil, a truly terroristic plant. I had a heavy walk-behind mower and decided I would get rid of them. On my first day of that project, I mowed right into a clump of the unwanted plant and found it more disagreeable than expected. A swarm of large red wasps were not of a mind to have their home torn up. I turned my mower loose and took refuge in a horse stable. Those wasps were so vicious, they wouldn't let me have my mower back for several days. Finally, I bought a pesticide spray, and they found that so objectionable that they flew away. I heard them all singing, "I'll Fly Away." Coffee weeds were also a menace. I never could grow delicate plants that started off as weaklings, such as carrots and asparagus. The weeds would choke them out before they could get a foothold.

In the great snowstorm of 1973, I think it was, the animals were dumbfounded. The ground was covered in eighteen inches of snow in open space. In banks, it was deeper than that. The children and I walked over to the farm, for we didn't dare try to drive. We found the cows standing out in the stuff and the smoothness of the surface around them indicated that they hadn't moved all night. Icicles hung from their ears and noses and other parts. Finally, we got them into stables, several in each stall, and the cowed cows soon felt the ice leave due to body heat. As we drove them from the snow, I felt a heavy thud hit my shoulder, and I knew cows didn't fly. It scared me *bleepless*. It was a cat that had been sitting on a fence post waiting for a warm surface on which to land. From that time on, until it took up with a nearby family, the cat jumped on my shoulder every time it saw me. I usually let it stay, whether plowing, fencing or mowing.

After we got back home that day, the children took Rachel's tv-trays over there and slid down the hill on them. Tough on the trays, but very good for the children's morale.

Just one time did we ever feel that we couldn't handle the workload. That was when I brought home eleven bushels of peas late one afternoon. As we sat down to shell and process them, we glanced at each other with weary eyes and shook our heads. The next day, I loaded the peas into my truck and hauled them up above Eatonton to get them shelled. A man up there had a pea-shelling machine. Since everybody who planted peas had a bumper crop that summer, nobody in Milledgeville could shell them for us.

On the way home with my produce, I would drive by Guy Smith's filling station for gasoline, for my little Gravely garden tractor and for my truck. That twelve-horsepower Kohler engine in my Gravely was better than my mule that had only one-mule power. Guy saw all my vegetables as they came by and deemed me qualified to be a member of the prestigious Progressive Farmers Club of Baldwin County. He got me in, and I was secretary of the Club for at least two decades.

To summarize my part and Rachel's in farm activities, we did not grow, freeze and can vegetables during the years I was so heavily involved in Rotary work. The land was already in Lin's name, of course, but he would have welcomed me to garden if I had been able to find the time. We held on to several shelves of Mason quart jars until we moved from the large house on North Columbia Street. At that time, we gave away more than seven hundred of them to various agencies and other friends. So many jars were hard to place, but we finally had no more quart jars! They reminded us that in the heyday of our canning, we had often run two seven-quart pressure canners simultaneously until far into the night.

As mentioned earlier, Lillian's primary interest in the land was a place to keep her horses when they were not in summer use at Camp Gwynn Valley. In due time, she became director of the riding program there, a position she has kept until the present time. We would pull those horses, sometimes as many as thirteen or fourteen, over the mountains to the camp and then back at the end of the summer. Some summers, Lillian and I both nearly went broke feeding the critters. Occasionally, hay was scarce, or "scase," as we had said in Lickskillet. We could buy it locally when it was available from brokers like Guy Smith, otherwise we had to go out of town. One summer we had to travel as far off as Loganville, Georgia. I rented the largest U-Haul and we went up there and we brought it back full of hay. Believe it or not, we had fun doing that.

Vivian's interest was primarily in the small animals like bovine calves, but she also loved the horses and helped with my gardening. She joined the other children in great sympathy for any animal that was sick or lame. They kept one calf alive through early morning and late afternoon visits when they were in college. One night, they thought the calf was dead, and they all cried about it. The next morning it had resurrected itself and was eating the feed left in the stable, just in case of a miracle. They later sold it to a friend in North Carolina, where it eventually died of a heart attack. It was as if a family member had died.

Evelyn was my helper in gathering vegetables. She and I still laugh about one incident related to picking green beans. The variety of beans known as Contender beans would bear forever if it received the right amount of rainfall and other care. Rachel insisted on saving every bean. If the bean stalk bore them, pick and can them! Late one summer, she inquired as to the state of the bean stalks. Who knew what was coming? We had already canned what seemed to be about one hundred thousand quarts of beans!

Green beans don't freeze well, so not a bean had experienced cryo. I told her that a few beans, here and there, remained in the garden. I neglected to mention that the few referred to three rows, three hundred feet long. Rachel dispatched us to gather and bring into her kitchen as many as there were. Evelyn and I knew that there were two or three bushels on those rows, so we left the house with heavy hearts. We picked for over two hours, but when the sun began to sink below the western horizon, Evelyn looked at me and said, "DADDY, what are you doing? I said, "I'm pulling up these *bleeped* bean stalks, and we are going to tell Mama they have quit bearing. We did just that! It was several years before we had the courage to tell Rachel we had squandered the bounties of nature. We know where she is, so we'll look her up and apologize once more when we have "crossed the bar."

Lin loved that twenty acres with a passion. When it became evident in the early nineteen- eighties that my Rotary duties would prevent me from taking care of the place, Rachel and I deeded the entire property, barn and all, to Lin. His sisters had all agreed. He was really thrilled, and soon he bought a small house trailer and established it on the highest point. I think I have neglected to say that we had electricity run up the hill to power lights in the barn and a pump in the well. He had the electricity extended to his trailer. He spent much time there, and when avascular necrosis required a hip replacement in his early thirties, he used his "farm" as a quiet place for recuperation. At all other times, he hosted many parties there and was praised by guests for his culinary excellence and social grace.

He still owned the property when he died in 1990. Then, by agreement with Rachel and our three daughters, it was again mine. As I walked the land, memories of Lin and the blessings he had been to Rachel and me overwhelmed me, and I asked God to take care of our boy. I kept the site of those memories for about three years and then sold it, never to view it again.

The nineties were tough years for Rachel and me physically. Her health was deteriorating precipitously, and I developed prostate cancer. For my description of my treatment, see "News and Views," an unpublished pamphlet.

What had I gained from owning land? Let me count the ways (here I am mindful of Elizabeth Barrett Browning). I enjoyed seeing our children happy over there, doing what they wished unencumbered. I enjoyed seeing Rachel sitting in the truck or in a chair watching me work. I enjoyed seeing her gaze at the flora and fauna, at the growing vegetables, at wildlife that appeared out of nowhere, red foxes, deer, rabbits, quail, wild turkeys, and many others. The deer were marauding pests and should have been thinned out by at least seventy-five percent, but that would have been ugly and unlawful. One year, we had two of the healthiest rows of lady peas ever produced. The deer mowed them to the ground overnight. I nearly *bleeped*. Yet, it was an atmosphere we had discussed and coveted many times in earlier years.

What did it mean for me personally, other than a bullet hole in my leg? We came home from visiting my parents on my 49th birthday. It was late, but I wanted to gather some turnip greens before dark. I grabbed my pistol because wild dogs had driven me quickly into my truck the day before, and that was unsatisfactory as far as I was concerned. I began to strap my pistol on but somehow the holster had become unfastened. My pistol struck the floor on the hammer at such an angle as to plunge a bullet through the calf of my right leg. That was unsatisfactory too, inasmuch as it changed my plans for the afternoon. The bullet had gone through without hitting the bone, had passed dangerously close to Lillian's head, and lodged itself somewhere in the ceiling.

I grabbed a clean towel, wrapped it around my leg, and requested a driver to take me to the hospital emergency room. I went to the car. I sat and sat. Nobody came. Rachel, Lillian, and Lin were frantically looking for a set of car keys that were at various places in the house, just not visible. Of course, I had a set in my pocket! Finally, a set was located, and I was transported to the hospital and placed on a table to die, I suppose, for a doctor barely looked at the wound and left. When the doctor from Augusta, who was helping in Milledgeville that weekend, got back, he asked me whether I had brought the bullet with me. I thought that a rather silly question. I knew he needed it for the police, but was I supposed to catch it before it lodged in the ceiling, or go upstairs and bore holes in the floor until I found it? I said, "Man, I didn't stay over there looking for a bullet." He took offense and left for another while, left that jerk lying there!

When he came back, he asked me whether I had brought one like the one that went through my leg. I thought it best not to infuriate him further. I simply looked at Lin and asked him to run home and get the doctor one of my bullets. He did. The doctor left with a disdainful look at the silly *bleep* on the table. About two hours later, my personal physician came by. He inspected my wound and dismissed me with instructions as to how to treat it. Of course, many rumors coursed about town. According to them, we had an argument, and Rachel shot me. Or I was out on the farm hunting wild dogs, and shot myself. Perhaps I had tried to commit suicide and failed. I cannot even remember all of the rumors, much less repeat them. It has been a long time since my 49th birthday, and I am old.

One ramification of this event was that Rachel got furious with me. I was shot by my pistol on Sunday. The next day was a workday, and Rachel was to drive me the one block from our house to the Georgia College campus. Oh Zeus. The battery was deader than Hector, and, believe me, that man was dead. Read all about it in Edith Hamilton's *Mythology*. I grabbed my walking stick, and, in spite of Rachel's tearful pleas, I walked to work. I regretted that. Oh, did I regret it. She convinced me that I was, indeed, a stupid *bleep of a bleep*. When she was sure I was fully persuaded, domestic tranquility was restored, and all was well on the home front.

When I returned from work a bit early that first day after Rachel shot me, or wanted to, our Pastor, Rev. Rembert Sisson, and a group of prominent Methodist laymen were there to see me. They laughed about the rumors and the very fact of the puncture itself. Our children were furious that those men would laugh. As a matter of fact, I laughed too. It was uncharacteristic of me to shoot myself!

The reader who is still awake will recall that a few pages ago, the question was what land ownership meant to me. I must confess that I digressed a bit to discuss the unwelcome hole in my leg and a larger hole in Rachel's bedroom ceiling. I kept my pistol in her closet, because she had more room to conceal it there. Incidentally, the hole in her ceiling was still there when we sold the house. It was there to remind me that I had come close to killing myself, or my oldest daughter, or both.

The real meaning of our land ownership to me was that I had proven my original conviction. The God of the universe was out there in the open with us. Now I am not a pantheist or even a Rousseau or a Thoreau. But I do believe that as Jesus defined the God he served, "God is Spirit," (John 4:24), and I believe that Spirit is in the quiet places of his creation. I believed that a prosperous relationship could be established between the Divine Spirit and his creation. As I look back now, it is amazing beyond any reason that for more than a decade my garden consistently produced enough for summer fresh vegetables, with some left for winter canning. Even in the dry years, there was always something, not everything, but something that made our efforts worthwhile. Now, I don't have my head in the dirt, maybe just in the dust. Sometimes, the desert will not "blossom as the rose," but I must be thankful that I proved my point to my satisfaction. Given the total circumstances of my existence for the past eight decades and more, Dad was right when he said, "Son, you can't make a living farming." Under more favorable basic circumstances, I now know I could have. Selah.

Maybe I am too selfish in my evaluation. I suspect that what the land meant to us as a family was a closeness that transcended all other benefits. The six of us loved it separately for one reason or another. Collectively, it meant an enhancement of the family fellowship as we sat around the round oak table. Spiritually, that was the value of our land ownership. Selah.

FAMILY AND RETIREMENT

FOR SOME REASON our children grew up, all graduated at Georgia College, as the former Women's College of Georgia came to be known, and then they left home. They all married, our oldest having run away and marrying at age twenty-eight. Lin's marriage ended in divorce, and we invited him to return to his upstairs prenuptial quarters until he could make whatever other arrangements he might choose. He did, and he was still living there when he died. Rachel and I were happy to have him there. He was good company, and besides, he could keep the squirrels out of the attic and the bats out of the chimney! We dearly loved his genteel company.

Vivian married first, by a few months. She and John Wesley King, Jr, were united in holy matrimony at the First Presbyterian Church in Milledgeville July 9, 1974, just after he graduated form Georgia Tech. He was soon admitted to the medical school at Tulane University in New Orleans, where he achieved an outstanding record. His medical practice is now in Milledgeville.

CROSSING POLECAT MOUNTAIN

Lillian married Christopher Watson Ware on December 23, 1974 at Pretty Place, South Carolina in an open-air pavilion atop a mountain. All the mountain folks had long underwear and wore it to the wedding. I didn't have any, and thus didn't wear mine. It was left in India because of weight. By the time the preacher said, "Who gives this woman away?", I was shaking like the proverbial dog that had eaten too many persimmons, seed and all. The congregation assembled thought I was unusually emotional when I said, while doing the St. Vitus Dance, "I, her father do proudly give her away." Very proudly!

Now, I have never been recognized as a professional photographer, rightly so, but an amusing phenomenon occurred at Lillian's wedding. Two professional photographers took pictures that day, but the ones I took, amateur that I was, were the only ones that came out. I suppose the professionals were either shaking harder than I was or were frozen in place. Lillian now teaches in Searcy, Arkansas. Husband Chris is a wildlife manager for the State.

Evelyn married David Winston Dooley December 2, 1978 in Bone Chapel at First United Methodist Church, Milledgeville. The wedding was in a heated chapel, so I didn't get cold. David is a retired teacher, and Evelyn is a microbiologist.

All except Vivian were married by Rev. Edward B. Nelson, Director of the Wesley Foundation in Milledgeville. Vivian was married by Rev. John Campbell, who at that time was Pastor of First Presbyterian Church

I should say a bit about our eight grandchildren, Dargan Maner Ware, Gregory Linton Ware, Rachel Meghan Ware, John Wesley King, III, Leigh Carrie King, Helen Lynn King, John David

Dooley, and Rachel Lee Dooley. But it occurs to me that I should let their parents do that when they write their memoirs! Our grandchildren were a great joy to Rachel and me and, of course, still are to me.

Time went swiftly by as Rachel and I did our jobs. Each morning, we would arise, grab the covers on our respective sides of the bed, straighten them, rush to the kitchen for a quick bite of breakfast, and be off to deliver the children to school and ourselves to the workplace. Rachel was a good cook, having learned the art at the feet of her mountain mother, and could cook up a great meal in no time at all. My twenty years at Georgia College (now GC&SU) were gone so quickly that it seems now as the time elapsed between tomorrow and today.

I must record here that during our working years, we found many opportunities to take brief tours of Milledgeville and learn of the rich history of the city and Baldwin County. But for one to have a chance to see it all, I recommend a taxi tour.

I locked my keys in the car at the Post Office parking lot recently and had no spare key in my pocket. That deficit has since been remedied, but at that time I was up *bleep* creek without a paddle. I went at once to the city library to seek a friend to take me back to my apartment for a spare key. That particular friend was not there. She was in another library, in which she should have been, for that's where she said she was going when she left the lunch table at Café South. I asked another friend who was working in the city library that afternoon to call a taxi for me, a favor she graciously granted.

The taxi arrived in front of the library within five minutes. I entered the vehicle and stated my desired destination. We started.

Then the driver stated he would have to take a lady up North Columbia Street a piece before he could deliver me to my apartment. He added that it was on my way and would not delay me. We proceeded to Dogwood Apartments. To that point, we were going in my direction. The lady came out and announced that her appointment was in Hardwick, several miles to the South. That was just so many miles in the opposite direction from my Villamar apartment. The lady reached her intended destination safely.

As we rode back toward town, the driver informed me that he had one more customer to deliver before he could get me to my desired location. He said that it was out North Jefferson Street, right on my way. When we turned right off North Jefferson, we entered territory that, after my forty years in Milledgeville, I had yet to hear of. I hope nobody ever asks me to take them there, for I don't know where the hell we went! It turned out that two ladies, not one, were in there to be served. We traveled far enough to reach Madison, Georgia and still were in that maze of roads.

At last, we emerged onto North Jefferson, and I was truly on my way. One hour and a half after I expected to reach my destination, I was at my apartment. I secured the desired key, and we returned to the Post Office parking lot without additional interruptions.

The driver charged me eleven dollars for the tour.

Soon, Rachel and I realized that we were very tired. It was time to retire from gainful employment. I retired in June 1983. Rachel worked two years longer and retired in 1985. We desperately wanted to have that honeymoon we had never had, but we didn't exactly get that. Instead, we found great satisfaction in service to mankind through Rotary International.

At first, I fought the proposal of several of my fellow Rotarians in Milledgeville that I allow my name to be placed in nomination for Governor of District 692 of Rotary International (southeastern Georgia, roughly encompassing all Georgia clubs within a line from Augusta to Macon to Valdosta). When we looked at the list of other candidates, Rachel and I agreed that I wouldn't win anyway, so I let my name go forward. Something happened! By the time the nominating committee got to the moment of decision, I was the only candidate left. The others had withered away in light of my scintillating personality! They didn't know me from John of Patmos, but they just knew what a fine fellow I was! Oh, I forgot. One fellow had not resigned. He was pushed out and was mad as hell at me for winning. In fact, I was mad at myself for the same reason!

Prospective Governors are trained at an International Assembly and elected at the annual International Convention. My Assembly was held in Nashville, Tennessee in early 1985 at the Grand Ole Opry Hotel, and my travels with Rachel resumed. My local Club made it possible for us to attend. If I didn't attend, I couldn't be a Governor. That was understood at the time of my initial nomination and all members of the Club were wonderfully supportive throughout the three years the governorship encompassed, Governor Nominee, Governor, and Past District Governor.

At the Assembly, we met many international men and women of Rotary. Women were not yet in, except as wives of their more illustrious husbands! That didn't deter Rachel from having one of the most wonderful times of her life. The hotel was so large that she could not nearly walk to the sumptuous international meals and other suggested places, but we had taken her wheelchair. Often, I would have to literally run to get her from one place to another. With my coattail flying and Rachel scared to death the front wheels would hit a crack and lock, we met every event on time.

Many more journeys were to come for Rachel and me in my Rotary service. Those included conferences in Kansas City, Missouri; Lexington, Kentucky; and Las Vegas, Nevada. In Lexington, Rachel and I chanced to be in an elevator with the President of Rotary International. Always the gentleman, he motioned me to go out first. I rushed to obey and ran Rachel's wheelchair right over his neatly shined shoe, with Rachel in the chair. Of course, his foot was in the shoe. I apologized with great obeisance, fearing that I would be the first Rotary Governor in history to be fired from volunteer service. He assured me it was just fine, that he was not hurt—as he hopped away! He is now deceased.

In Las Vegas, I encouraged Rachel to sin. She had always wanted to pull one of those levers on a slot machine, and I saw to it that she got to do so. We budgeted twenty-five dollars to that enterprise. After several pulls on the lever, she had fifty dollars. After several more, she had nothing, as it was planned at the foundation of the world! There were many glances from fellow gamblers. Perhaps better said, there were many gawks as they saw that gray-headed lady sitting in her wheelchair jerking that lever! To me, it was one of the great scenes of our marriage. But I was doomed, for I had caused my own sweet wife to stumble (Jer: 18:15).

Sadness was beginning to overtake us. Rachel's health began to decline precipitously in the early nineteen-eighties. She had much difficulty with problems related to menopause, often hemorrhaging without warning and needing to be given medical attention at once. When we began our Rotary District travels, this became embarrassing for her and a hindrance for me in discharging my Rotary responsibilities. Her needs always were foremost. On a Rotary mission to Jekyll Island, it became necessary for us to rush back to Milledgeville at once to physicians who knew her needs. We made it in time! A neighbor gentleman came to our home after two or three days to find out what was wrong that she had to come back to Milledgeville so quickly. He insisted, demanding to know exactly what was wrong. Pushed to the ultimate, she told him. His face would have set the whole block on fire! And he indicated that if that were happening to him, he probably would have rushed back too!

Her health continued to slide downward. She began to have bouts with pneumonia requiring hospitalization. During my year as District Governor, 1985-86, she had such an attack in mid-fall. We were out on a visitation schedule and were in Blackshear, as I recall. Had it not been for our son, Lin, I would have had to resign my position, and such mid-term resignations have always thrown the District into confusion. But all I had to do was call Lin, and he would come in the middle of the night, if necessary, to pick Rachel up, take her straight to the hospital, and get her admitted. I would finish my duties and return shortly thereafter to relieve him. He was truly a "gem of purest ray serene." (See Gray's Elegy... read it all!).

I wrote my Club Presidents that Rachel and I had made one of the toughest decisions we had ever made. She could no longer travel with me, but I would do my best to finish my year. They understood. Spring came, and she got stronger and was able to attend my District Conference with me. It looked as if her physical stamina might strengthen.

We continued to attend district conferences. I was still a Trustee of the Georgia Rotary Student Program, Inc., and travel was involved. A meeting was scheduled to be held in Thomasville, Georgia, October 6-8, 1989. We made plans to go. On the morning of the sixth, she felt nauseated. I picked up the telephone to call the chairman and tell him we would not be there. She begged me not to do that, at least not until about noon when she might feel better. By noon, she assured me that she felt much better and that we should go. I was not sure, but she insisted and we journeyed to Thomasville.

Not long after we registered at the Holiday Inn, she took a shower and lay down for a brief rest prior to the scheduled banquet. Within a minute or two, she looked at me and said, "I am having severe chest pains." I called the front desk immediately. A person, title unknown, came to the room, listened to her heart, and called an ambulance. After the confusion of looking for what she might need in the hospital, I learned that she had been admitted to Archbold Hospital. The desk personnel were able to give me understandable directions to the hospital, quite a few blocks distant, and I went there.

Rachel was still in the emergency room when I arrived, but she was on the way to being sent up to the Cardiac Care Unit. The emergency room doctor asked me for a name of a doctor in Milledgeville he could call. I gave him the name of our son-in-law, Dr. Wes King. Whatever the emergency room doctor told Dr. King, it caused the latter to ask to speak to me. He said simply "Linton, we will be there as soon as possible." I gave him directions and then went up to the door of CCU. I was not permitted to go in. I stood outside the door for several hours, hearing repeatedly the technician shout, "Breathe, Rachel, breathe!" She didn't want to breathe, but she pulled through the night, and a number of specialists had been assembled.

Dr. King pulled the family in from their various places. Lillian flew in from Arkansas, Vivian came down with Dr. King, and Evelyn came from Lilburn. Evelyn's husband, David Dooley, stayed at our home in Milledgeville to answer the telephone. There was trouble waking Linton III from his upstairs bedroom. We didn't have a very good doorbell, and what we did have could not be heard by someone sleeping upstairs. Finally, a friend threw pebbles up against his windowpane and got him to unlock the downstairs door. His friend later revealed that when told of his Mother's condition, he sat on the couch and sobbed, but soon was on his way to Thomasville.

When the family assembled, the cardiologist in charge gave us the news that Rachel probably wouldn't live. The outlook was that the darkest hour that is said to come just before the dawn was about to appear momentarily. But an excellent team of professionals had been assembled, and slowly they brought her back to the point she could ride to Milledgeville. Vivian followed me back. Our station wagon was comfortable. We met at agreed upon places and helped our "precious cargo" get a little fresh air and go to the bathroom. We got her home. All thanked God for that wonderful team of doctors who had saved her from the ultimate.

I immediately resigned all my volunteer positions and began to concentrate on watching for any signs that might indicate Rachel needed medical attention. Many of my friends couldn't understand such a move. But, as they say, I was "on a mission" to help keep Rachel alive as long as humanly possible. An especially good Rotary friend in Jacksonville, Florida called to upbraid me for chickening out on Rotary. Arrangements for Rachel could be made (like a nursing home). Of course, they could! Rachel remarked often that she would never object to being in a nursing home if the family thought it best. My stock answer was, "As long as I am able bodied, you ain't going."

Eight months after her Thomasville experience, our son was dead. He died July 1, 1990 in a one-car accident. The car was his pickup truck. He had plunged off a bridge, and both he and another young man were killed. Later estimates were that they were not found for twenty hours. Nobody looked for Lin because he often stayed overnight at his farm. The news, brought to us by our daughter and son-in-law late at night on July 1, was such a stunning blow for me, and especially for Rachel who had so recently nearly lost her own life. We often found it impossible to eat our breakfast because a glance across the table would bring us to uncontrollable weeping.

Very soon, 1991 I think, Rachel began to have pains in her back, quite severe. The diagnosis was gallbladder trouble. At the suggestion of Dr. King, we rushed her to Piedmont Hospital in Atlanta where the surgery was performed. Since she had long had a lesion on one of her ovaries, surgeons and she agreed that while they were "in there" they would remove the gallbladder and the ovary at the same time. The incision was long.

Before the surgery was actually performed, she was offered the option of "backing out." Her doctors explained that she had only a thirty percent chance of surviving the surgery, that she could go back home and spend a couple of months enjoying her family, that being the maximum time she could expect to live without the surgery. So, they said, we recommend you take the time at home. She decided quickly to brave the odds, hardly any odds at all in her favor, but she pointed out to them that she had survived the Thomasville nightmare and would gamble on this one. She won!

We, her family, wept with joy. I quipped that of her 2000 body parts, she had only 1998 left. She vowed she would limp along on the rest of them. Once again, her life had been saved by good physicians. She gave credit to Dr. King for his loving watch and for knowing what to do and who could do it.

Her health continued in its downward plunge. We moved from the nine-room house to a six-room house, because she could no longer negotiate the steps from porch to ground and didn't trust me to handle her wheel chair, with her in it, down the rather steep ramp we had installed. The smaller house had a flat on-the-ground entrance/exit. She liked that. She could have a garden on the patio and get out there and work in it. She watched the birds, listened to their songs with intense interest and otherwise observed nature. We had a large back yard at our new abode. Several times, I drove the car to that back entrance, then drove her around the yard so she could see all the flora therein.

We still had many occasions to joke and laugh with each other. Friends wanted to know why we had moved "at our age." Instead of rehashing the unvarnished truth, I told them in Rachel's presence that she had aggravated me so many times about dusting the books upstairs, that I just sold that house and bought one where she could see the dust on everything we had. I begged her not to get pregnant, remembering that, in our younger years, every time she got pregnant, she dug up the whole yard and planted new flowers. She never lost her sense of humor. Hope was fighting to get out of Pandora's box, and we did everything we could to assist. It continued to be obvious that Rachel was losing strength. Careful watching and careful manipulation of her medications by her doctor, Dr. R. John Barrett, kept her going. It was touch and go. A "GI Bleed" in 2002 nearly brought the end, but she snapped out of that on borrowed blood.

As she became less and less able to take care of herself and her household duties, I tried to take over, with some regrettable stumbles, like the time she asked me to zip up her dress. It was a side zipper, and I made a mighty pull! The zipper moved upward until it hit some flesh. There was pain all over the house, and I was summarily dismissed. I was duly repentant, but, I felt, not completely forgiven.

I began taking over tasks such as operating the washer and dryer. She was reluctant to relinquish those duties, but circumstances forced us to adjust our priorities. Reality was closing in. She did not give up her positions as Chairman of the Board and Chief Executive Officer. That was all right with me, for I didn't want those jobs anyway—too much responsibility. She told me in detail which garments to wash together, which this and which that. I obeyed, and all seemed to be going reasonably well. However, I had not learned well the operation of the dryer.

One day she was in bed all day. I was in my office, having discharged my utility room duties to the point of starting the dryer. She was in her bed across the hall. We smelled smoke at about the same time. The smoke alarm complained. Now, where in *bleep* could the smoke be coming from. I advised her to be calm, that I was checking the problem out. Finally, I worked my way to the utility room. Fuzz was flying everywhere. I reported to Rachel that I had turned off the dryer. She wanted to know what was wrong with the dryer. I reported further that it had been throwing fuzz around and smoking. She inquired, "When was the last time you cleaned the filter?" "WHAT FILTER?" falls within the category of questions a husband should never ask. A woman gets pretty much agitated when she is almost smoked out of her sick bed by the mistakes of a dumb mate. I apologized profusely, and domestic tranquility was restored.

Other events occurred during our final years together for which there is no explanation except old age. There are conjectures but no definite answers. I conjecture that my brain is so heavy that it sometimes blacks me out and throws me down on the floor, or whatever is under me. This time, it was the kitchen floor. I had gone there to take some early morning medicines and had a glass of water in my hand. At least my memory is that it was water and not some kind of detergent picked up in my stupor. My great brain took a vacation, and I took a tumble. I know I did, for I woke up on the kitchen floor in a contorted pose. I gradually got hold of a counter, pulled myself into a chair, and in due time to a shaky standing position. Then my addled brain brought my attention to the fact that somewhere in this episode I had a glass of water in my hand. Now where in the nether regions could that be. I looked all over the kitchen, looked and looked some more. My quest for the unholy grail turned up no clue. It simply was not in the kitchen. So, I expanded my search.

The den was adjacent to the kitchen, but the glass could not possibly be there. I reasoned that the overhanging cabinets would have caught it before it flew in there. I looked anyway. It was there. I had somehow thrown a curve. All logic was trashed, and so was the glass. It had settled in the den to the left, smashing into Rachel's stationary bike, a Sears "Tailwind" version (appropriately though indelicately named). Shattered glass covered the carpet in that area. Then I thought of Rachel. She rode that bike every morning and soon would be in there for her exercise. I activated the vacuum cleaner to save her bare feet. I had just about accomplished my goal of cleaning it all up when she appeared.

"What are you doing operating that thing at this time of the morning?" she wanted to know. I replied meekly, "Sweetheart, I don't know."

I prepared our cereal for breakfast, and gradually poured out my story. She couldn't wait to tell our daughter, Vivian. Before I knew it, Vivian had loaded me into her SUV. and we were on our way to Emory. A young doctor of impeccable reputation looked into my head, saw nothing, and dismissed me with, "Sir, if you were my father I would tell you to go home and take an aspirin a day for the rest of your life." So far, I have complied.

My bout with prostate cancer hit in 1996. Rachel insisted on knowing what was going on in the treatment. I wrote daily descriptions of everything that happened during my thirty-five trips down to Macon for radiation. Each time, I couched the most serious information in humorous language to cut the edge off her worrying. When all was said and done for that summer, 1996, my PSA count was down to .03 and all seemed well. Rachel was happy. She said, "I think I went through all this pretty well." I said, "Sweetheart, you were a basket case." We had a good laugh.

As we moved into the 21st century, my back went totally nuts, and I went to the hospital for a few days. In the meantime, Rachel had reached the stage that she couldn't walk at all, and the bathroom doors in our dream six-room house were too narrow to accommodate her wheelchair. We had to have a place with wide bathroom doors. Our son-in-law and daughter were generous and took us to their home for an indefinite period, at least until we could find a place in which we could live independently.

It is amazing how many builders don't think of older citizens when they build. It took five months to locate a suitable place. The builders at Villamar obviously thought of the elderly when they built. Just before we moved to Villamar, we bought Rachel a scooter and she had a pleasant time with it in wide doors and hallways until she died.

With Lillian, Vivian, Evelyn, and I standing by her bed, our loving Mother and Wife died April 28, 2003 at 2:40 p.m. Rachel and I had witnessed her father's death in Chatsworth in 1941. Now, almost exactly sixty-two years later, her immediate family witnessed her own.

In closing these bumpkinish episodes, I choose not to speculate on matters eschatological. I accept the statement of Paul in his famous explanation of the Love of God. (I Co: 13-12). Even John of Patmos, in my opinion, was looking through rather opaque glass.

As one who spelled Shakespeare "snake spear" for the first fifteen years of my life, that is, until I had crossed Polecat Mountain, I shut these accounts down with Shakespeare's *Sonnet 104,* one of his sonnets called to my attention recently by a very dear friend. I should have quoted it to Rachel upon my return from India and updated it each year to sixty-one. Selah.

> To me, fair friend, you never can be old,
> For as you were when first your eye I ey'd,
> Such seems your beauty still. Three winters cold
> Have from the forests shook three summers' pride,
> Three beauteous springs to yellow autumn turn'd
> In process of the seasons have I seen,
> Three April perfumes in three hot Junes burn'd,
> Since first I saw you fresh, which yet are green.

CROSSING POLECAT MOUNTAIN

Ah, yet doth beauty, like a dial hand,
Steal from his figure, and no pace perceiv'd,
So your sweet hue, which methinks still doth stand,
Hath motion, and mine eye may be deceiv'd,
For fear of which, hear this, thou age unbred;
Ere you were born was beauty's summer dead.

My sweet mountain shrub, we'll meet again someday. It just can't be otherwise.

To Rachel

We've had a long journey together, about as long as a second. But my memories span each paved stretch, and each rock in the road. How sweet are the memories of the plain places, and of our triumphs over the rough ones. I can say "goodbye for now" no better than Henry Wadsworth Longfellow has already said it in his "Delia."

Sweet as the tender fragrance that survives,
When martyred flowers breathe out their little lives,
Sweet as a song that once consoled our pain,
But never will be sung to us again,
Is thy remembrance. Now the hour of rest
Hath come to thee. Sleep, darling; it is best.

Meet me, as we have agreed, on the steep side of Pine Log Mountain. We'll scale it once more, forever.
I love you, Sweetheart.
Linton
.

About the Editor:

Dargan Ware is the eldest grandson of R. Linton Cox, Jr., whom he knew as Pop. He is honored to be able to present his grandfather's work for publication and share it with anyone who may be interested. Mr. Ware is a consumer protection attorney, poet, and novelist in Birmingham, Alabama, where he resides with his wife Kristi and teenage triplets.

He is the author of the novel *The Legend of Colgan Toomey*, which is available on Amazon. He is currently in the process of publishing his second novel, *Old Soldiers Never Die*.

Mr. Ware may be reached at authordarganware@gmail.com, @ManerWare on Twitter or on Facebook, where he is the only Dargan Ware in the world as of November 12, 2020.